Reflection

Ian G. Thomas

Summary

Reflections From the Mere is a collection of poetry and short stories addressing a broad range of subject matter. The poetic pieces take many forms, from short and simple rhyming verse to more complex rhyming patterns and also free verse, while they address many areas: ***the history and future of human kind, nature, politics, education, childhood, human nature, emotions, the 'self' and religion***.

The exploration of these areas is sometimes approached from differing perspectives and occasionally contains conflicting viewpoints. Some reflections are personal interpretations of established philosophical theory, both ancient and modern, often attempting to place them into modern day life and events. The short stories attempt to expand some of the subjects and ideas into contextual settings with a little more complexity.

It is hoped that by avoiding the categorisation of the pieces into topic areas by chapter heading, as well as adding some variety in approach, the reader will be encouraged to reimagine and reinterpret them, to use personal experiences and thoughts and possibly create new ideas. **The overriding purpose of the book is to establish a practice of philosophical consideration of all areas of the modern world.**

Reflections From the Mere

Copyright © 2024 Ian G. Thomas

All rights reserved.

ISBN: 979-8-8619-7685-5

CONTENTS

Acknowledgments   i

1 S   **P4**

Anatomic Harmonic Pt1
As We Played Heart Shaped-Hide and Seek
When I Text My Sister
The Crossing
Birdlife
Quotes and Memes
The Child's Story
The COP26 Finale
Chains of Gold or Daisies?
One Day and the Next
Regrets
Time's Relative
Sold As Seen
The Yellowing Leaves
The Knives
Jubilee
One Yellowing Leaf
Now is Not the Time
This Rocket-ride Life (Theist)
This Rocket-ride Life (Atheist)
Prescription
The Creeping Silence
Lighthouses, Satellites and Statues
Death's Door
Autumn 2020
A Medieval Goblet
Forest Needles
By the Old Colliery
Towton Battlefield 29.03.1461
The gentle Rain

Paper Podium
The Bird Cage
Pavey Ark, Great Langdale
More News
Worst Fears
Dirty Paws
April15 at the wooden Bridge
Categorised (A Re-wilding)
Jet Stream
A Heaven-Like Place
Acquisition (Waiting for the- Flood)
False Dawn
Three Gods
The Bus
Fledge
The Church at Wasdale Head
An Idyllic Walk in Heaven-
   and Hell
The Bat
The Boat will Come
It Used to go Like That,
        Now it Goes Like This.
The Old House
Newspaper
Yesterday's Blue Skies
We Westerners
My Largest Possession
Dead Man Walking
The Light Goes Back
In Search of Space and Time
A Walk Towards the Grave
Coronation Day (May 6th 2023)
One True Friend
Mission
These Young Lives
25 Years Ahead
Your Experience is Over

2 M   Pg 33

Anatomic Harmonic Pt2
This Big House Where We all Live
Out of Time Pt1
Out of Time Pt2
And on the Last Day, God…
Harvesting: Shipwrecks
Harvesting: A 70's School One Monday
They Write Their Names
House of Mirrors
The Web
Perfect Copies
The Penguins
Outside the Gates
    (The Lockdown-Easing of May 2021)
Tomorrow's Towering Tombstones
Just Stop the Bullying!
Seven or More Lives
English and Proudish
The Kids These Days
London
Harvesting: Otley Street
Kelham
The Dead Calm New North Sea-Coast

3 L   Pg 59

The Wheat and the Wildflowers
The Waiting Room
Deep Inside the 6 o'clock News
A.I.
The West
Momentary Bones

The Supermarket Sweepstake
'Gable'
Re-Wilding
A Walk in the Woods
New Year's Eve
Harvesting: A Path to Where?
Humans: Organised at Molecular -Level
We Don't Get Rain Like We Used -To
Trickledown Tarn
Ghost Writer
Reflections From The Mere

4 XL   Pg 120

Cathedral of Sand
(Pg121)

Seed Sower (The Boy in the Shed)
(Pg133-167)

'The Author'
(Pg 171)

ACKNOWLEDGMENTS

Great writers and the inspiration they provide.
The lockdowns of 2020/21.

CHAPTER 1

S

Anatomic Harmonic:
Part 1 (Our Lives Together)

Each note of a beautiful tune.
Seems so empty and alone.
Each second of a perfect day.
Comes together in the same way.
Each letter of a moving story.
Takes its place in poetic glory.
Each starling in chaotic creation.
Is in a symphonic murmuration.
All the microscopic parts of our lives together.
Aligned and synchronised in time forever.

As We Played Heart-Shaped Hide 'n' Seek

...among the pain and lies. The millions I counted. I searched the Earth, raked the forest floors, swept the clouds from the skies.

I searched the atom bomb beaches and the trenches. The tooth lined fences and the cathedrals of ashes. The landfill debris and the black bubbling sea. The desert sands. Behind cavernous staring eyes and in the magician's empty hands.

It was the darkest day. The stars came out and they gave you away. The words I'd said I now regret, 'you better hide so well to protect you from the creeping doom' when again we finally met, I never thought you'd be hiding behind the moon.

When I Text My Sister

...about TV sport or something or other.
Work related or just the weather.
There's a back-catalogue within this messaging.
An infinite trail of images and feelings.
Flowing deep within this latest chapter.

> First school week, first school: catastrophic.
> Transferred to her class to ease the pain.
> Make the whole thing a bit less traumatic.
> A Christmas morning's endless laughs.
> The old garden, spring over the wall.
> A sledge that floated down cloud white paths.
> Or down the road to collide with a pole.

These coloured jewels I can recall.
Given time and concentration.
But they simmer somewhere in all.
Our latest communication.
A crystal mist in the atmosphere.
Fossils of a distant year.
Like graphite dust or pigments on paper.
A silent, sub-atomic whisper.
When I text my sister.

The Crossing

From where I sit, I see the message flash on screen:
    Part of the paperless dream.
The chaotic desk lies beneath.
    A grey group of pixels power out.
        From the page, unseen.
I see false realities in red, blue and green.
    The list, books, far-fetched plans.
I see the next meeting fall through my hands.
    Yet here before me is the stream.
Beside the password protection of the cattle grid.
    Here is the grass and the quiet air, so clean.
Where the lambs were well hidden.
    In the long-desired retreat.
But I remain in a battleground.
    In the gap where we meet.
Transition from the tortured tail.
    Of the mouse and the trap.
        And the constant tap-tap.
A search for truth at the cross on the map.

Silver flames fire up from the waves.
Into my blind eyes.
And on the breeze birds cast their chorus.
Into my deaf ears.

So, to make the crossing out of the shadows and scale
the pass from the market town's hunt for food.
To Eden Beck's skies of real blue and the real pasture of
real green, the tranquil ground's gathering of truth.

Birdlife

Nesting, shark-like in an ivory seat.
A kingly nest of feathers and the dead.
Bright delight, morsel of meat.
Sleeps soft in its unmade bed.

Seeking a lifeblood of not spider or seed.
A treasure for two princely heirs.
Many full days so the babies may feed.
All will be lost if caught unawares.

Apex hawk in a seat of power.
Masked predator, preying at alter.
A dove's survival delivered by the hour.
Another day without falter.

Quotes and Memes

Kind and caring, beautiful phrases of 'how to live a life' we are sharing.
Copying, pasting, posting golden quotes we are wasting.
The dagger and the sword of modern life on a silver and bloody plate we are serving.
Hacking through our lives, our own beautiful advice we are not taking.

The Child's Story

She sat down a while.
On the wooden bench, bravely updating her profile.
She can't ignore the stench of the toilets as she watched the train leave.
Round the bend, slowly. Like where he went, God bless him, tattoos of hate with hearts underneath.

She turned to look into the waiting room of the station.
Seeing only a dirty window with her own sad face in.

'This is it then, it's just me,' she thought.
She picked up the things she bought and walked down the platform.
Lost and alone in the hostile world she's been placed in.

In that story she wrote, in school, there was only love and laughter.
This wasn't in the story in the child's head, this terrible chapter.

The COP26 Finale

"This place needs a clean," someone said, putting down his 18 stone on his labelled seat.
"What do you mean?" said a man in big shoes and a painted-on smile, "we should just, maybe, eat less meat?"
Our man walks in, flan on his face, makes up some story about winning a football match or a race. He wipes dust from the table and says, "It's a minute to midnight but we just pulled back two goals!"

The crowd watch the scoreboard in disbelief as VAR reviews. It rules out the goals, the team was off-side. Oh hell!
Now they wait for the whistle. Or is it the bell?

Chains of Gold or Daises?

Walk through modern life's bitter cold.
Rings run round our souls.
Treading graveyard paths painted foolish gold.
This is what I'm about:
    Few more pounds, then I'm out.
    Before I get lost in the bloody wheels of industry.
    To leave alone with the ghostly wheat behind me.

One Day and the Next

One day I walked...

In the woods: The forest's beauty.
Breeze sweeping.
Trees leaning.
Life-breathing.
Commanding and protecting.

There's everything here.
A forest half full but full.
Beams breaking through branches.
Penumbra enchantment.
Berries like beads.
In heavenly hair.
Flowers chime up from the providing leaf.

Next day I walked...

In the woods: The forest's treachery.
Wind cutting.
Trees creaking.
Life-bleeding.
Commanding and rejecting.

There's every fear.
A forest half empty but empty.
Shadows lurking like trenches.
Umbra entrapment.
Blackberries like barbs.
In deadly wire.
Vines climb up like the stifling grief.

Regrets

My best friend at school, well, for a year or two: His mum worked at a sweet factory.
I didn't make the most of that opportunity but it's not a thing I regret.
Things I can't even remember. Things I thought I would never forget.
That's what I regret.

Time's Relative

Not money nor glory can lead me here.
A moment here is an hour elsewhere.
The flaming ferns, bathed in the autumn sun.
Spring shoots of hope, have become.

Sold As Seen

Who could explain the drops of time?
The salt sweat and the carbon-conscious elements of the Earth.
The parasitic worms looting their host to within moments of desolation.
Springs new desires to leave the praying mother.
Spreading the ridge to the mountain top, this budding foresight.

A new day and with the darkness of the abyss.
Or a new dawn?
Our salt and ash become rocks in the grave clay.
Our footprints pressed in peat, are the birth of new Gods.
The ultimate feat. What are the odds?

The Yellowing Leaves

Seeking escape into mild and yellow years.
With creaking timbers under bulging sails.
Filled with structured time's relentless deadlines.
Looking to gather the canvas and cease the battle call.
To conquer the lucid life once and for all.

The Knives

Noble sculptors: Tall-standing knives.
Creating and carving.
Shaping theirs and others' lives.
Hunting beasts and threats.

Cutting the meat, the seat, the path and the bed.
To cut a path again and again.
To catch the tears shed.
For a life of few cares.

Jubilee

A monarchy in a minor key.
'Kings or Queens anybody?'
'Oh, on some things, minor things maybe.'
Mugs and towels mainly.
Poster framing, coins and keyrings.
A corgi with a crown, inflated or let-down.
Garlands, napkins, monarch pale ale, all's for sale.

One Yellowing Leaf

One leaf on a windy day under blue skies, leaves the fruiting march early.
Two seasons in fully green attachment end suddenly.
Three simple wishes for a long and coloured fall.
Four full seasons to be met in all.

Now is Not the Time

In love's lost halls.
In eternal contentment.
Energy: Free from fear and the untrusting mass.
Not the time to hold her hand.
To caress it in both hands.
To sweep the innocent cheek with rear-view fingers.
To whisper words to 'heaven'.

Now is not the time, when these moments arrive.
The time was when she was still alive.

This Rocket-ride Life (Theist)

This rocket-ride life.
Launchpad so slowly left.
Accelerating, the view appears.
The edge of space nears.
25,000 miles per hour at time of death.

This Rocket-ride Life (Atheist)

This rocket-ride life.
Launchpad so slowly left.
Accelerating, the view appears.
The edge of space nears.
17,600 miles per hour at time of death.

Prescription

Those who lay upon the river bed.
Who see the small waves trickle past as crashing waterfalls.
Watch the Sun pass, fast as fleeting clouds on windy days.
Those who live on prescription.
Who don't paint on walls.
Spiral inward around their own graves.

The Creeping Silence

Some such creatures would extract their souls
Lay them to momentary rest
Sores bleeding on the market's fiery beach

Some rest theirs among the hills
Or on the still-warm tiles of rooftops
Under the moon and out of reach

Waiting for the creeping silence
Then listening to the aching whispers
Pleading for peace, they preach

Lighthouses, Satellites and Statues

Blue, brown and green.
A picture of a lockdown, I have seen.
It's a story of experience, truth and lies.
A story of irony and how it works in real life.

Death's Door

Joseph had never even seen the main track to town, his waking moments chased by fears of the crown.
Fortune, she fell for the spell, such was her age and her character as well.
From Fortune today, Mother saw no frown.
The gallows shake and the bodies break.
Joseph watches these men's fates.
Fevered desires buried in the fires, Fortune turns to hate.

Autumn 2020

And this year's leaves are many.
And this scene, by any means, takes our breath.
With its solemnity and not its beauty.
And this year's deaths are many.
And this autumn scene reflects their death.

A Medieval Goblet

What time are you from? The moments feed new ones, our time is fed by others and will in turn. At this moment we arrive all infinite in line. On a wave on the shore that shapes the sands of time and forms all future lands. On a wave we are a moment, a life or lives.

Forest Needles

The needles will hide with the autumn sun.
Find them and find the time that is gone.
To fight that baseless and false present at last.
That 'now' time and own it full.
Find the needles, find the details.
Possess them before they pass.

By the Old Colliery

The miners strike at the magnetic movement.
Forges a change and the red is in mind.
They feed on and stoke.
A sleeping seam of an ancient time.

Tire of transient ways and dismiss the collected view.
Welcome the new.

Towton Battlefield: 29:03:1461

"Dispatch!"
The sky, frozen, holds for me, every sound in its path.
The spirt, fallen, screams out 'dispatch'!
These hands, open, pulling in the earth's blood.
These senses pray for redemption in the cool, red mud.

My form lies on the earth, I see from the skies.
Affirmation lies in my clouded sight.
Death cries to my senses but they somehow rise.
My mind now flies into a free but wretched flight.

In these dying times, I see more than all the things I have ever seen before.

The Gentle Rain

Ah! The gentle rain.
It sends me echoes of all that it touches.
A fusion of each silent collision.
Sent from these grey summer skies.
Ah! The mental pain.
Becomes free of my tensioned clutches.
An explosion of senses, make it their mission.
And react to a sound I now hear with my eyes.

Paper Podium

The drunken banter-bums are in the pub today.
Seeking nothing more than to piss-take their lives away.
Modern marathon men vie for position on a podium of paper.
Cometh the hour, forgotten tomorrow, the one-liner to savor.

The Bird Cage

The time card breathes its last for two days that will soon pass, hunted down by the latter hours of Sunday.
The cage door swings open but the bird inside looks frozen until the drinks ring the evening bells of Friday.
The new morning's light can tease a bird into flight onto the cold and wired canopy.
The wings come to life but the fear will contrive to seal this bird to its familiar territory.
The time will pass until the days start to last and the hunted retires from the fray.
The bird will fly and break through to the blue sky to render the cage just a memory.

Pavey Ark, Great Langdale

On top of the world and yet humbled beneath Pavey Ark.
The spread of the word brings spirits seeking free paradise.
Heavenly grey, rocky backdrop for a summer play.
Carving memories in stone: images to last all our days.

The climb, its pain, sweat and heated breath.
Is now just a staircase, floating and laden with beautiful gifts.

More News

Beauty and calm: Merely a prelude to ugliness and war.
The elegant ships we sailed on: Gunboats at our shore.

Worst Fears

He's late and the roads are cold and wet.
She sits worried at the table, set.
The wine is open, he called when he left.
Into her mind, the darkness has crept.
He's late and would never not call.
She knows now, deep down, he's nowhere at all.

Dirty Paws

He's late and not even called.
She's wanting just a sign.
He's late and not once has he told.
Her that he's close by.
He's late and she's had the odd cry.
But he appears: Fur wet, young eyes closing, dirty paws.
Needing the warm and dry.

April 15 at the Wooden Bridge (The Warm Breeze)

For a few moments, now and then, the trees wave.
In the warm breeze.
Something tiny dances violently on a slender thread.
The line of a web.
In the warm breeze.
The long grass, nettles and various weeds and leaves.
Spring back and forth.
In the warm breeze.
A Red Kite! Distant and still against the sky.
Flaps and miraculously holds steady.
In the warm breeze.
And the middle of the page is reached.
The top corner lifts slightly.
In the warm breeze.

Categorised (A Re-Wilding)

Bringing only bashful looks
Self-preserving and lost
It's who he thought he was
Swimming among the hooks

Bringing no boastful books
Self-serving with a cost
It's who they thought he was
Trapped and taped inside a box

Stacked and labelled with a class

Like a fossil lies alone
It's who he will become
Screwed under exhibitor's glass

A cog lost on the factory floor
A categorised entity
Starts a fight for destiny
A search for the dark-room door

From deep in the night's lies
Starts a chaotic flight
Like a firework's lights
An explosion in the mind's skies

Jet Stream

The graph line curse comes and we suffer in its trough.
The dreaded curve we helplessly exist above.
A battle we rarely win cos of a geographical sin.

A Heaven-Like Place

Late night conversation, half of us drunk, how has my life been? Oh, the ups and the downs! The sorrows I have drowned, but it's healed now, the scar you found.

True contentment, not solitary, nor confinement, even in union, no claustrophobia, no isolation, desperation or resentment.

This latest phase, feeling like a passing to a better place, another page, another verse, another world or even universe.

And before I pass into the air, this final phase I anticipate with delight. With you, in a heaven-like place.

Acquisition (Waiting for the Flood)

This is not a walk in the park, this is a sneak in the gloom and dark.
A seep through the veins, a dopamine dream that, once awake, is real and remains.
The relentless acquisition performed at the altar of a restless disposition.
Looking back in time at the unchained ones, too distant now to find.
At jewels in the past, like stars in the blackness, our eyes are cast.
But seeing nothing, a void, a chasm deep and unforgiving.
The precious link is gone, the gap is deep and the time too long.
A river of sacrificial blood brings gifts and will one day bring the flood.

False Dawn

I can survive as I console my own mind with petty priorities.
I can hold my breath long enough to believe in them.
I can cross my fingers and still see my own demise in wishes.

I can deceive my soul and call it my kindness.
I can release no scream, like a muffled mouth in a terrifying dream.
I can speak of my freedom: that lies only in my mind.
I can take a moment or an age from any random life as they from mine.

Three Gods

Owner of the three Gods: heart, soul and mind.
In a war-ravaged dot in time.
Science is taking millennia to eradicate religion.
These warriors, each immortal, know their enemies as well as themselves.
In turn, they rise and fall.
One will lay in blood but will rise again.
In time, milk and blood flow in equal measure.

The Bus

A puppet with invisible strings
A machine programmed at birth
Thousands of generations: repeat, repeat, re-print
Trial and error for better for worse
The technology and the science: the inheritance
The giant's shoulders
The bus improves but not the passengers

Fledge

The finest and slenderest twig, these branches, this tree.
Climb out to the frosted air.
And there: make your own step.
To where no one would dare.

The Church at Wasdale Head

Deep within my own mind, a precious memory I'll always find.
One left between the green fields of lambs and the blue skies above.
One cast in love.

An Idyllic Walk in Heaven and Hell

A viewpoint, a picturesque spot.
A beautiful calendar shot.
Walking in late summer's fields, autumn trees heavenly and alluring.
Walking in late autumn's fields, winter trees and bushes burning.
Hear whispering winds fan furnaces, stalking.
Black barn, charred branches and logs.
A hooded hoof took off through here.
His men crawling behind, eager to please him.
Human unkind, cramped and scorched.
Attacked by infection and itself from within.

The Bat

Oh! There's a bat. Dark on the sky. Fleeting. Wing beating by. There's a star. Bright on the sky. Light burning. Beam passing by.

The Boat Will Come

On the river, time ripples by.
The storms and the calmness.
Random cycles and swirling pools.
The crests and the troughs.
Build up in the blood of its heart.
The beat will come.
To this place on the river.

On the river, time ripples by.
The boat approaches in the last.
Shadow of the final wave.
In deep trough, the shiver.
The boat will come and cannot miss.
On the river, its swiftness to wonder.
Is all that there is.

It Used to Go Like That, Now It Goes Like This.

I don't talk after midnight.
Once the shadows dissolve with the light.
The darkness buttons its coat, wipes down its sleeves.
I occasionally watch, read or just think. Mostly sleep.

I don't like to drive in the dark.
Or in winter.
Or while anyone else is driving at the same time for that matter.
I don't like counting down days but occasionally still do.
Or taking those risks, like in a car, on a bike, or hillside.
Worrying what others think of me: I don't do that now, but I used to.

The Old House

Looking from the quietest of narrow roads.
This solitary house: Derelict for as long as I've known.
But behind me on the opposite roadside.
Never caught my eye: A pair of pillars stand separate and alone.
Once the entrance to the house, now flanking a field of wheat in lines.
These two brick figures like infant gate-keepers.
Waist height in a wall of more recent times.

Newspaper

Places demons in my head.
Bitter and twisted words are said.
Places rocks in my hand.
Builds empires on sand.
Plays on the cells of our time.
Leads the wake in line.
Divides the mass in two.
Splinters the many and then the few.

Yesterday's Blue Skies

Still clear in my mind, yesterday's blue skies I see.
Picked from the days like a wild bloom of beauty.
Today's grey skies only heighten that memory.

We Westerners

We Westerners.
Nobody seems to hears us.
For we must surely be buried.
Under an avalanche of goodness.

My Largest Possession

The house comes in second to the life I was given.
It's more than the house could ever be.
I own both now, but the house has cost me.
About 400 monthly payments taken.

My life isn't worth what it was in those early days.
The lifespan of the house is far superior.
It's aged better too, interior and exterior.
If I had the receipt for my life, I could maybe take it back
but come to think of it, I got it from a rentals place.

Dead Man Walking

...was said by the guy beside the convict.
On death row.
On the journey to the chair.

Condemned man.
That pour soul.
Facing the end.
We are all that man.

The Light Goes Back

Teetering on the winter years.
Remembering where green time has gone.
Though the trees are full, leaves are yellow and the branches black.
Hiding away this Saturday when the time goes back.

In search of Space and Time

Spend some time away. Somewhere nice to take my cage and let the waves take the days.

On a road in search of somewhere that buries time.
Deep in the ocean, over the horizon line.
The restless sun of June warms the endless days.
Memories that disappear under time's hungry waves.
Resurface like a whale at sunrise, a soul it saves.

A Walk Towards the Grave

You walk along the warm, late-summer beach, hearing birds singing in the dunes.
Heavenly tunes.

You walk through the cold, dark winter night, at the end

of the corridor, you arrive.
Ward number 5.

Coronation Day (May 6th 2023)

Two hours to a new King, it's 10am.
They're waving an empire on a short, plastic stem.
The crown is on, pushed down hard so not to slip.
Unthinkable! Not so much with this weakened grip.

All types on the streets, joyous scenes, everyone you could possibly meet.
Laws recently changed, thrown into baskets, bursting into flames.
Many gifts handed over. Oh! what a show. Oh what, another!?
History reveals itself from under its 20th Century cloak of concealment and cover.

A weathered statue on shifting sands.
Eaten by modernity and time, in ever more alien lands.

One True Friend

Gatherings are a tedious affair for me.
The pleasantries, the gratitudes and the over-exaggerated 'how are you doing?' and 'long time no see' attitudes.
That talk is shallow and even when the drink kicks in it has nowhere to go. It hasn't the courage to swim to the deep end, it just sticks with what it knows.
'Maybe you can only truly live in peace once you've

fallen out with everyone?' Or so the thought goes.
I'll sink deep within and fix on my relaxed eyes. Walk across the thin ice and remind myself of the safety signs. "Hey, haven't seen you in, like, two years!" "Yeah, it's been nearly five but only two were mine!"
A singular contact is a meaningful one. Shallow, waist-high or deep and sometimes all at once. Others are a train full of sleep, mostly dull, 'take it or leave it' and ankle deep.

Mission

An unknown mission we are still to become aware of. We are the universe but is its mission one of self-awareness? Ultimately to control itself? Is it trying to gain some self-control? To stop the tiresome bouncing? Or is it beating and breathing?
Ours is to become 'immortal' and then, as the universe, to achieve the same.

The goal of the game, at level 9 of 10, our capabilities still small but in time we are close. On the brink. We've been filling in the pot holes all this time, not knowing the road we're on.

What if we are the closest part it's got?
And what if we are not?

These Young Lives

The lambs and their petrified mothers
Ewes, scared but so brave
Left to the early spring frost
And their own devices
To emerge into the glory of summer
On the roadside beyond the fences

25 Years Ahead

I see his pain.
You have to look for it.
He's not one to complain.
He's walking. Leaning. Crouching.
10 steps behind and 25 years ahead.

Your Experience is Over

Waking up in a very strange place.
"Memory recall could take 4 days.
You have a 93.4% chance of full memory recall.
Partial 1.4%
Zero 5.2%
You agreed to the experience: 'Human from the old 1960's onwards.'
Thank you."

Reflections From the Mere

CHAPTER 2

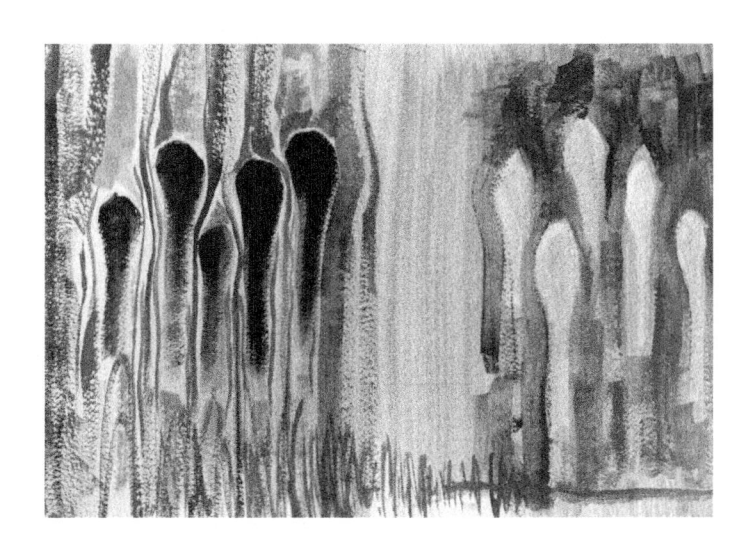

M

Anatomic Harmonic: Part 2
(A Grasmere Ensemble)

The stone bridge of this ship will endure.
To look deep into such moving waters.
The Hydrogen sons and Oxygen daughters.
Alone and flowing in a paired adventure.

A search for paradise inside a cool spring day.
On a mercurial canvas of infinite size.
The artistic scene will be customised.
Onto the hills beyond the lambs that play.

Seeking perfect days among resting travellers.
By fires, nesting under autumn's roofs.
Or in the chapel café, on time-worn pews.
And on to Rydal without horses or carriages.

Once golden trees adopt budding beauty.
Removed from the world, between the lines.
Reading in the bookstore's lost times.
Or in the windowed bay of tranquillity.

The curators bury memories like nuts in the earth.
Painting the numbers and rooted in confusion.
Seeking answers and truths from an illusion.
Then presenting exhibits in a piece beyond worth.

In the theatre the act stars a mocking storm.
Moments are notes, unrecognisable and yet.
At the falling of the sun, the symphony is set.
A masterpiece is revealed as the curtain is drawn.

The water flows randomly from river to sea.

The yellow leaves flashing in the air.
Are caught as they fall and saved from despair.
Where the chaotic soil makes the perfect tree.

With a set design to make a day.
The seconds of the day will each play their part.
Then fly like starlings in the shape of a heart.
All perfect in their own way!

Commit this pure vision to a scrapbook mind.
And all its wisdom and emotions fused.
Assemble and align the particle views.
The memories in harmony are as one combined.

The view from the bridge down to the stream.
Patterns pass through undiluted meanings.
The hydrogen senses and the oxygen feelings.
Conjure into pebbles, the stones of our dreams.

This Big House Where We All Live

There's a whole man who works between the floors.
Sings songs, then he's gone.
He's familiar with all the stairs.
Most question if he cares.
But he can talk to anyone.

There's a couple in the hallway of the ground floor.
Heads on pipes of condensation.
Blackened walls of fate.
Cans of food out of date.
Poor non-relation.

Some live further down, in the cellar with the rats.
Spare coins tossed in a hat.
They all fell on the wrong side.
Nowhere to hide.
Former proletariat.

First floor, mostly open-door and still warm inside.
Has the best view, upstairs or down.
Not too much resentment.
They've got home entertainment.
Things are worse on the ground.

Some look down from the attic at the top.
Or look down at penthouse plans.
With blue skylounge thinking.
Champagne drinking.
How the gold coin lands.

They can only see through to the next floor down.
Offices of dictation.
Lives bought and sold.
Computer controlled.
Administration.

The house functions when there's no floor overfilled.
It's the house we've made.
With all its varied apartments.
For our great achievements.
It's the price we've paid.

Out of Time (Part 1)

A child of a fading age opened the summer door.
    And like the turn of a page,
    Saw the same free day as the ones before.
A child oblivious to the moon,
    As it clattered by, spending dreary nights on
wet and windy steps.
Far from the sleepy eyes under curtain skies.
With no desire to see or hear,
    The evidence of any engineer.
A sleep so free under watchful eyes of the night.
And the sleeping world waits, to wake in unison,
    To the angel sun.
And out on skipping feet or wheels fast down the street.
The end of the day and the dark door closing.
    Feels weeks away.

Rest in the mercy of this waiting world.
On warm fields and in the trees.
Strip bare this stick of bark and leaves.
Green handed with an old but shining blade.
An even more ancient tool is made.

The song that whispers in the mind,
    With the fire smoke that lingers into the night.
The arctic circles the summer's day,
    And knows nothing of the night,
        Or the embers no longer bright.
The Earth would spin so slowly.
Mindful of any mindlessness,
    It would gladly stop occasionally.
The bells of school are buried,
    Deep in unmarked graves.

And yet the church so old skips by so mildly,
    Marking no time,
        With a gentle blink of golden beauty.
Running so bold and wildly,
    On paths, up steps and down roads.
Relatively moving,
    So fast and holding time,
        In ribbons and bows.

The summer would return and would not be new.
The same one to savour again and again!
And the summer long would travel with me like an old friend.
Carried in its arms or outside of time to fly.
It would not have such rudeness to just flash by.

Out of Time (Part 2)

        The same moon I see tonight.
    In elegant and heavenly light.
It falls freely, gliding down the darkened skies.
Guiding me madly to the distant hills,
    Of grassy earth where time flies.

I was free and open as my mind could be.
        Now I'm free as my mind will let me
            And closing daily.
Sleeping starlings in the whispering trees,
    Already longing to be carefree.
I wander the fields of posthumous victories.
And this crimson self-portrait devours the time,
    The blood of my wishes in every line.

Head down the white-water thread,
>   And among the time-patterned rocks.
>   >   Call out for the long-lost trickling dream.

I was carried on time's spring shoulders,
>   Now deadlines march towards me,
>   >   In their tick-tick monotony.

I'm dropped under the march of its winter feet.

I can see the moon and stars bathed in glory!
Only now, in time's unforgiving speed,
>   I see life's beauty,
>   >   And watch from outside its great contradicting story.

I long to feel the time stop on that summer field.
>   Or the same summer return to me.

Those moments are a mirage.
>   A work of fantasy.

...and on the last day, God...
(An A.I. Pre-Cursor)

Here he comes, Adam, lonely on a cold, dark day.
No dilemma or temptation.
Nothing at stake.
It is the end of his time.
Nothing left to take.

Flawed and trapped, like in a jar.
What id what we saw was just like soil in pots?
Climbing up to feed on stalks.
Only to return to the dirty bed.
Bones picked over too, for all our empty days.

There were no false dawns.
There were no big days.
Egg shell eyes and egg shell ideas.
Just the one basket, not well hidden.
Its wicker wasted and weathered.
Boiled eggs in a pot.

Leaving just a note on a post.
The black, bitten fruit and the honey.
Into the shadows this ghost goes.
Into the deathly valley.
Leaving hollow stones, fossil feet.
Leaving glass beeches.
Satisfied smile now out of reach as we die in the alley.
And the golden trenches.

Harvesting: Shipwrecks

I sit down and talk to you here.
The first time for about 25 years.
It's the first time ever, without response!

I forget the greying grass around me.
The rapid Sun, the same one.
Connect neural channels that remain.
Find faint lines in my book of time.
The bright moments of happiness and shadows of pain.
I forget the seconds I still have.
How they're now spent measures my love of life.

I contemplate the near-infinite odds with which you put me here.

To me, you were always old: aged from the first day of my memory.
Yet here I am, aged little in my own mind.
But to the same degree as you when my years were only three!
The moments I find are like small boats on the sea: loaded with treasure.
I seek the ones I misplaced: all now beneath the waves.

Your boats were sinking so fast when I visited you last. I came with too little. It was not me, in my right mind that you saw at that late, late time. A vast expanse of ground had manifested from the time between our births.

Your century encased you, brought and destroyed you. I have two and a chance in each, of equal measure.

I have destroyed the first. It didn't slip from my hands or fall, like sharp sand, between my careless fingers. Its canvas was blank to its death and I've torn its paper memories to pieces.

The second is mine and I see it clearly. I use some of its time to repair the pieces before it destroys me.

I slip through time's darkest corridors, going silently back with no pictures on the walls or text on the page.

I sit here and think hard, bending time right back to the corner of Otley and Burgoyne as I take that small plastic car from your hand of middle age.

Harvesting: A 70's School One Monday

To wake silently screaming in a bed safe and warm.
A dark morning before the winter dawn.
Dropped down a well all the way from Sunday Heaven.
To black Monday hell of the playground bedlam.
Deep, terrified breaths in the over-painted corridor.
Rigid as a corpse behind the final door.
Fearing the relics of an ancient hour.
To be taught a lesson in the strangest manner.
Allocated seat, pencilled in for all to see.
No pen, not yet neat and too care-free.
'Work through these and bring them to be checked'.
Summoned, having taken too long, I expect.
In full view right by the desk, under the stopped clock.
Awaiting verdict in the dock.
Don't look into the death-dog's judging eyes.
Mathematical monster, flaming fury and graveyard ice.
Hit by the full force of the corporal law before my peers.
Sat shaking, awaiting a break-time of tears.
Walking home at the end of the day.
Felt like Tuesday was a universe away.

They Write Their Names

        One hot summer I wrote out my name on a wall using tar from the road with a lollipop stick in my innocent young hands. By the age of ten I'd lost little of it. I think I still have quite a bit left. My innocence survived well, but not as well as my name in tar. Forty seven years later, it's still there. Looks the same as it did then. That child has gone, but not that far as its innocence lives on.

A baby is born of pure innocence like pure energy into a world of matter. And there is so much the matter with the world that the innocence is dissolved by it. For some, a little and some a lot. People become manifestations, distortions, mutations. Criminal constructions.

Sculptures formed from machinery of a thousand years. World leaders and influencers, many of who have so little left, add to the matter in the world and the matter dissolves more innocence.

Conscience vaccinated, pills for humility.

Sacrificed under a knife of ancestral surgery. A name on an arms deal just 55 years after he learned to write it. A name, just like the small boy, the same name, the same human being.

A name to make father a Lord. A name to burn a city. A name to ignore the law in their own courtroom.

A name starts a war to protect a political ideology or maybe to protect land, or at worst, to protect a personal legacy. Serving only the dopamine queen, he who once wrote his name with innocent hands.

We cannot mistake innocence for a lack of experience. Meet them: In their night on their mountain top, guide them along the treacherous ridge to redemption. Then forge a path to cajole the innocence to the salvaged summit. Taught well and raised up to lead.

House of Mirrors

What's real and what's not in a dreaming visit to the old school? There was a stranger standing there in its place. Its ghost was there too and the building gone. All the ghosts were there and the others live on.

Some are lost on a road they found.
Some are found and some no longer around.
Some feel pain and some seek redemption.
Some seek nothing: There is nothing standing there.
Some seek the truth.
Some are many and some are one.
Some are gone.

I always thought we just knew.
Everything and we never really cared.
I now realise that we simply threw
Away the chance we all shared.
Now we all know the world and we feel it is there.
The conscience that grew, I hope the ghosts will spare.
I wonder if some were everywhere.
I wonder if some were ever really alive.
I find some light under the earth.
I mined the depths of my subconscious threats.
I seek rebirth and find new life.
I find experience, imagination and creation.

The Web

The dark minds bleed their endless feeds.
Planting seeds along downward streams.
Sinking in traffic clouds.
A gas of self-composed nightmares and not dreams.
Cutting contact with its earth.
Blocking, deleting and reporting.
No longer available, no longer supporting.
> Who walk a street below the sea, below the zero mark constantly.
> Who seek a light along their quicksand path.
> Who walk the night and not the day.

The time-beat keys are struck and never turned.
Sitting with sickness in their endless webs.
Spitting obscene on magic wand silky threads.
Like-minded strangers defending the sanctuary.
Barking mean at all that is said.
Breeding infections inside their own heads.
See group-think in heavenly deathbeds?
Or spun on trial and error with spiritual links instead?
> See the green, white twisted branches, not leaves.
> See winter's black trenches, not fields.
> See the cattle, doomed, not seeds.
> See the valley's black rivers, not peaks.
> See the tolling and fearful flood, not the gentle ringing bluebell wood.
> See the leachate crime of human grime, not the blooms forever climb.

Perfect Copies

Some are distant and removed to a universe away,
never to be reunited.
Some walk side by side.
All the while, we all live day to day.
Except for the 'can't wait' and the 'really looking
forward to' things we say.
We each have a parallel puppet, stringing through life,
everyone else's way.

We leave our true selves early in life.
We leave our clean selves behind as soon as we wake.
The false face is put on.
The nearest we get, it would seem, is the interrupted
dream we escaped from.

From an early stage we create perfect copies.
Contorted and mismanaged through time.
We develop them into increasingly imperfect copies.
Manipulated images: We have left ourselves and
stepped aside.

We do things we wouldn't do.
We say things we wouldn't say.
Refrain from things, ourselves betray.
Spending our lives as another person.
Trying to make contact with the original version.

By the time it feels possible to be ourselves again, just
who that was has been forgotten.

The Penguins

All to become just a fleeting visit.
To this land of hopeless glory, we see?
The remains of any future soul: Black, hidden and entombed.
Or with sunlight beams and lightning bolts.
In a weathered palm, go free.

All come to paradise and blindly walk past it.
Condemned to return to the womb of the sea?
From the lily pad basecamp of a short story.
Like Dodos conga to a blinding light.
The Easter men mine without worry.
Sail with a compass seized by a rusted fright.

A course infested with blight is took and we seal up the book.
Plotting and looking only for a walk in the park.
Finding fevered streets, damp and dark.
Looking for a way out with an ever-diminishing shout.
From a mouth of repose.
Seeping out and unheard.
A timid crawl to the shores.
From paintings in caves early dawns.
The slow march of the flightless birds.
Down paths with high, bullet-bitten walls.

The bird of tiny wings, it still sings.
Songs of ambition and blind intent.
Songs of past glory and precious moments spent.
And with its short wingspan of attention.
Could yet be back to the sand, sent.
Darwin weeps for the birds and their wings.

Some would frown upon such treacherous things.
A God would look upon the delicate fledglings.
That some might fly to far, glorious lands.
That they still have their destinies in their own hands.

Outside the Gates
(The Lockdown-Easing of May 2021)

Packs of dogs are tearing at the flesh of their beloved capitalism.
Seeking thrills, quick and easy, wrapped in their own shallow, fake fur of hedonism.

The shameless hunts are 'wearing' thin.
The skin-deep mirror sees nothing within.

Tramping through re-built cities, miles from the heart.
These city streets once sliced through with blades, now sheathed.
Over pulsing beats and bloody rhythms of an ancient art.
There are fights now for new honour: mating calls, worthless positions, mythical new social orders and new religions.

Money heals human kind's bleeding heart.
Not fortitude or soul-searching. Not the inner workings of the mind.
Money buys them a place on the golden funeral cart.
This new, calculating and reckoning butcher of a God.
Will seal them to a new, mass-produced, die-cast, golden cross.

Tomorrow's Towering Tombstones

These walls are not weathered by fast-changing climes.
Not bitten by wind or dyed by the dimmed light.
The steel still shines where not covered from sight.
These are not monuments or historical finds.
Not sand-covered stone temples of ancient times.

Recent pulsing arteries fed towering brains, that fed bodies and not souls.
Palaces of productivity, they were tools in their own downfalls.

These were not built as the pyramids, castles, viaducts or cathedrals.
They quickly outlived their purpose like intricately designed stepping stones.
These are modern dinosaurs but still standing with new, green flesh on their bones.

They reached for the first world stars.
The arms of Plutus and the profiting prophets.
Their time in the fruiting autumn was a fleeting day.
Their time is gone.
Like a dying Sun.
But their battle was won.
It seems like yesterday.

Dust drips from the white wires.
Rust slips from around its smashed eyes.
Like tears, of the ghosts of forgotten years.

Just Stop the Bullying!

Secondary school was worse, before that it was just the teachers that were bullies! Ah, yes 1978 to 1982 the rules were different back then, there were fewer of them too, work was hard, no help, no time no understanding and disruption, wow! everywhere in that class that didn't help either. Break and picked for football, then not picked, not picked at all, shown the door instead, messes with your head. Things stolen and not just grades, expected 2 C's and got 6, worked so hard in that final year, could've done better if I'd done that for the full 4 years, oh and better working conditions! So kinda got through it, was worse for others, things I witnessed, it was depressing.
College, Poly, Uni all ok but Steelworks was a bit crazy at the start yeah probably some school yard bullies who didn't mature or maybe school yard bullied that switched positions when they left!
21 years teaching and not many bullies for me, oh no! Much better, well there was one maybe. Seen hundreds though and dealing with that felt constant sometimes, head of year for a bit too, sometimes it gets you down, sometimes reminds you and you try your best for that reason as well. But it's not my school, it's yours, the 21 years won't shape my life anywhere near as much as those 5 years shape yours, it's your school, your kids' school probably too, how does it make sense now? just stop! Oh, have things improved since '82? Well? When you do that, think! It's not just this moment you're acting in, you're acting through time. The effects could still be there days, weeks, years later and possibly for the person's whole life. 56 and telling you this story. 56,

that victim of yours could be telling their story! It's like you're still bullying them 40 years later, stop!

It's not my school, it's yours, mine was demolished: best thing for it. Here's my challenge, when you bring your kids here, be able to say 'this is your school and there are no bullies here. Why? Because we sorted it out. Me and my friends did that, we did it for us and we did it for you'.

Seven or More Lives

Teens:
Prime of life, private life.
Dreams and make-believe scenes.
Sacrifice.
Hidden face.
Hidden lies.

Twenties:
Theme of plenty, heart empty.
Passionless light.
Industry.
Life of automation.
Solitary.

Thirties:
Restful delight. Blissful flight. Life's glory.
Some crashes, stress, fights.
Log fires, forests and seeds.
Inflicted deceits.
Conflicting stories, lifeblood and gory.

Forties:
Take flight, lie and leave, just fly.
Alone and not.
Alcoholic tee shirts and flirts.
Morning walks to sleep.
Live night, dead days.
Working and acting, confident.
Fifties:
Contentment.
Heaven-sent in rested awareness.
Some frayed edges to dispel still.
Bliss, nothing to miss.
Not alone.
Home.

English and Proudish

The number 22 bus, disembarked on a journey through town. This wasn't a galleon ship on waves, ruled. Its passengers were not slaves, well not ones whipped into work anyway. They're a crew looking to plunder local land, not for treasure but coins for food and shelter.

He walks through the surrendering arms of the fly-over, aware of everything. A survival instinct when entering the battle ground. Some young men, like native warriors or defenders of the crown, glance over as they stand around.

Out from the darkness of an early winter morning. Out from the gaze of their cemented ways. Out from underground. Out from under the road, from underfoot, under glass, underclass. The shop windows shout his reflection: Vital images he uses for protection.

The mask he wears hides a purely native soul from the fearful, ignorant and prejudiced eyes. As he arrives at work again, he is under fire and under threat. He is a pure gold counterfeit coin, unable to pay the mythical debt.

The Kids These Days

Oh the kids today didn't see the snow, not like me, well, not in the same way anyway.
They never play, or do they? Don't live like I did, couldn't possibly. That would make me some kinda 'pass-on the baton' type and I can't do that hype, not for kids today, no way.
See we were better than them, better life, cleaner air, out there, in the smog streets, strangers we'd meet, unsupervised, uncategorised, no data, not in our lives.! Smashing glass on glass houses, bottles or glasses on faces.
Sun down, yellow moon we sang to a different tune, not these songs, don't have a tune and words we can't hear and can't sing to.
Oh mobile madness: Texting, texting, texting, always bloody texting, dancing, coordinating, reading, writing, spelling, researching, debating, evaluating, learning, creating.
Hit them I say, did me no harm but I did hit that kid that time, didn't deserve it. Or maybe I wouldn't be quite so angry, or No no it's not setting a bad example, not like that nob, that movie star on stage, hit that bloke, that's

bad, or the footballer, what an idiot, sets a bad example, always arguing and pushing people around, bully he is and earns too much as well. Should've been smacked as a kid. Or maybe he was!?

London

Central London escapes me. It appears to escape everyone.
The tourist from near and far.
The workers who drop anchor.
And everyone else who hates it or holds it dear.
None of them can really be here.

You should watch your backs, down with the screaming tracks. Most sit near the bar when they're on Tower Hill, if you sit near the door, stay on your guard and secure your bags.

The day starts with a battle for your attention.
The heavenly bells are sent to Hell by the drill and the siren.
Between giant glass curtains, the illusive winter sun.
It's not lit this winter ground since a war was won.

A thousand years are standing tall.
From the hill, showing everyone its brutality and beauty.
But looking north it's standing small.
Under the reflecting light of a new God's glory.

8am and at this hour, Anne lost her head at the Tower.
8pm and Sam's doing the same for happy hour.

The past and present power.

The church now sleeps behind the monumental towers.
The suits walk with pace, purpose and ample greed.
The polished tread from the heart to the head.
The limes are on the trees.
The dust is on our shelves.
The crimes are increasing out on the streets.
The justice for themselves.

So far from the solemn souls of the gallery gate.
The bank says 'yes' and takes its flesh.
With shoes to be shined, doesn't mind the wait.
Ladder to be climbed, standing on fingers.
He's doing well with all his eggs in all his baskets.
He sleeps well, unlike the ones on the slabs.
Colon, hyphen, open brackets.

Harvesting: Otley Street

Part 1

Is perfection in all its freedoms.
Is timeless afternoons.
Is a gift each visit.
Is a life with a limit.

Part 2

Playing at the old house about '73.
In the garden or kitchen, my sister reminded me.
We cleared the wall and it seemed we would all.
Suddenly be.

In the wilderness of our lives.
So care-free.

Part 3

Forward to the new house, it's about '91.
They still didn't seem old and it wasn't that long.
Drove myself over, it was a fleeting scene.
Was on my way to somewhere else, maybe.
She said, 'You've changed, since you've worked there.'
I laughed all 'knowingly' as I didn't care.
Told myself I'd created a warrior or something.
Maybe from my survival instincts.
A beast to battle with the curse of the men.
But did I really need to become so much like them?

Kelham

Rooted on a river down the valley from its sons.
Destined for industrial greatness in the wake of early innovators.
Now muted on the gentle and clear waters.
Witnessed by the modern workers and green branches.
The same spot of the Earth as the soot-covered drivers.

Firing furnaces and the rude awakening of hammers
ruled the land and its neighbours.
Inspiring creations like sparks from grinding wheels.
Inside the fight and the falling bombs.
Now forging relations behind a safety railing.
On block paving.
In culture cafes or out under the same sun.

Before the explosive youth, sat a child of watery wheels and mellow mills.
The air still flower-fresh, round the first, called 'Kelham Wheel'.
Now, in post-apocalyptic tranquillity, each turn of the ghostly wheel engineers people.

The people of community: the arts and the hearts.
On peaceful seats in park-like retreats.
Wildflowers full and hives house the busiest of bees.
The vessels and engines are redundant but majestic in retirement.
Standing proud of past glory.
Behind plaques and boards that reveal, re-tell or teach their story.

The Dead Calm New North Sea Coast

A spring morning in heaven
A blue sky painted sea
Praised inside a silent hymn
The singing fresh-water mirror
A symphony of the wetland
Resurgent in their new haven

Outward on the brave new North Sea
Beaten among the near isles
Floating, loveless on brown and green
Converted Lincolnshire lighthouse
A high-tide windmill in disguise
Deserted with a rotting tree

Calm tides on shallow waters ripple

Watched by the Moon they worship
Rising, swelling like a chemical reaction
The houses a maritime keepsake tomb
Their majesty rudely uprooted
As were their absent people

Who sold their denial burrows
For a patch of high moral ground
Outward, doveless to the viscous waves
Leather bound bible brown
Washing sandy softening the earth
Where buoys mark bungalows

Moving among the boatless dead
The burning age, woken from its bliss
By a phantom of its own provisions
Condemned to a new and nautical grave
A grandfather dead again in yellow weeds
An ancestral collection of bones and beads

CHAPTER 3

L

The Wheat and the Wildflowers

Verse 1: The Field

The morning mist hovers over their field under a polluted air and the time-measured spoils of a manufactured care.
There's richness in the soil and a birthing beauty that's uniform and 'fair'.
A bright future for the million seed that's planted free of weed and in balanced ground.
But the liberty breed, that's random, could lead to brazen and beautiful blooms where allowed.

Verse 2: The Wheat

In channels free of flower, the seed grows fast into the modified and nurtured tiller.
Standing straight in organised rows swept clean of infestations by a predatory killer.
The symmetry school stifles a heart and soul.
Ordered like tools and subject to strict controls.
They rise from the frost and stand tall in the drought of June: wave in unison and hum across the ground under summer's fertilising cloud.
The harvested kernels will pay their way.
Their stalks cut down in their grief and grouped to a sheaf. A bed of straw on which cattle can lay.

Verse 3, Part 1: The Wildflowers

There's a sense of isolation for the periphery plants.
They circle around the crowded, bread-winning streets.

Beautiful creations of natural selection, those not trampled by other young feet, their creative destinies to meet.

Verse 3, Part 2: The Cornflower

With a piercing blue pain and deathly hue, it knows little of a ticking hour.
Its story is well written and tells of battles won and lost. Fighting, sometimes in vain. Fighting injustices that beckon it, questioning its path again and again. The great communicator, telling of truths so that others may see. The great liberator.

Verse 3, Part 3: The Poppy

A blood-soaked seed, buried deep, is born. It takes the moral high battle ground.
It remembers the twigs swept away, the stalks and leaves raked ready for the spray.
Pushing itself up through the deathly earth and ties its colour to the mast, the full breadth of the battlefield surpassed.
Leaping at the new blue skies, an army of bloodshot eyes. Tearing through layers of entrenched minds to bleed its message to us: 'Remember'.
So that when it's gone from sight and the trench remains, its shadows still sway in the breeze of a winter day.

Verse 3, Part 4: The Oxeye Daisy

Each cheering daisy flower. Some small child that could be our saviour. Our worthy and virtuous influencer.

With petals of poetry dancing free and easy, tell the story of how we could be.
Refusing the torrent of make-believers, walking tall, engaging and trusting in our futures. Filter the fault-finders, the lies and deceivers.
We could now lose the abhorrent, parasitic feeders.
Rise, for our sake and lead us.

Verse 3, Part 5: The Many

Sweet Alyssum of full heart, Shasta Daisy resolute.
Cowslip and Buttercup, the Ragged Robin, the thistles.
Who are they and what could they become?

Verse 4: The Future

These beautiful creations still rise through the years.
From history's grey skies fall the coral tears.
Crystal eyes set on the faces of our fields.
Reflect from the skies and mountains like shields.

White Shasta, the lost-love daisy? The sweetest Alyssum? Yellow cups gather on their own yellow path in search of gold on a bow of colour.
What more can they do? Fed with fear and with nothing to lose and no time to waste, they forge a path from this vision-starved and striding haste.
Deep in the battlefields, creativity is merely 'tried'.
The world revolves around diminishing returns, where once it spun. Wildflowers are truly of the Sun.

The Waiting Room

The really strange part is, I don't remember the last guy coming back out. I'm sat beside the next one, waiting my turn, facing leaflets of guidance, symptoms and ailments, ways to get help and good advice. There's so many, I can't even pick one out. If I picked one up, I'd have to take them all. I'm not reading any of them. These places are worrying enough! The man is grey, quite frail and clearly been waiting a while. He has an expression of some concern that I don't find surprising. Seems patient enough and I assign this to his experience.

There are others here, both opposite and to my other side, towards where the door was. Most are elderly but two are younger and one is a child. An older lady stands out from the small crowd with her suggested smile and a glance around the room. It's so subtle it could be false but it's not: Her eyes projecting warmly like a treasured portrait. The younger ones appear less patient and it's evident to me that they are, as I am, busy people.

I have things I need to do. It's a busy day and my overloaded, supercharged head has been switching again, from one thing to another. The child and mother don't converse and this doesn't seem strange at first but does make me wonder. It takes my mind back to the man who hasn't returned, or the one before. I think the child must be scared.

I think there must be another exit around the back. It annoys me that I don't know this and that my journey here has been surrendered by my over-burdened memory. It happens a lot with my journeys especially on days like this. I need to concentrate more! My memory has numbed itself into a net and even my reason for being here has fallen through it. They will, I'm sure, let me know.

The man beside me gets up and walks to the obscured corridor. This is a relief to me as I can't be long here now. He must have heard his name called out, I didn't hear anything due to my mind wandering.

It's getting uncomfortable, sat here aching like I've sat here all my life. That's unusual: I've endured far longer in meeting or concerts but this pain is gripping me and this cushioned seat is now a stone. I even feel the seat with my hand and it still feels like stone. The room has become colder and darker. The rain outside is heavy now, sent by the darkness almost into the room and onto my painful brow.

The voices in my head are no longer my own. My name is called at last. He must have used the other exit. I get up, still aching, and any apprehension has been dissolved by the wait: I feel relief.

I walk through the kingdom of the hallway and somehow it doesn't even change my breath. I walk around the corner, stumble forward and at the base of my fall I see the same car right in front of me, the one I saw approach me as I walked in here.

Deep Inside the 6 O'clock News:
Oct 10th 2023

Story 1

The war the bombs the explosions and death for history, the madness and the misery we bring down on ourselves is news to me.
Coffee or tea?
The trickledown dream is a stream becomes a river, a lake that belongs to someone, another river, a deadly and poisonous sea.
Fighting, hiding, firing camouflage killing.
'The laws of war!'

Sociable like vampires. Parasites 'Massacre at the border'. Siege. Put the shutters up, pore through the rubble bare handed ground zero sign of blood they won't shut us up! 'Humanitarian law' in that report. A network of tunnels beneath the city, beneath all our cities all our feet, everywhere just waiting beneath, for us!

There's a tank, it's red, it's being driven by a crusading knight of shining armies over broken jigsaw pieces.
There's another tank, it's being ridden not driven its rider is pale and looking for new graves.
Board games.
Border games.
Bored of games.
Four tanks in all ride round this board. This time on the sand and one before was...

A Marching band and its bloody mindedness, still marinated in its own mumbling and muddied history. Under siege.
So, main news main outlet main educator main opinion-creator, proliferator. What's the story? What's the history? What's the future and what's the? It's not a Hollywood movie!
We're not telling you, too complex and complex viewing isn't compelling, look at the pictures.
Warning, you may find some images distressing.

An abstract thought: A Rocking chair, a bed something pulls away the curtain.
'who's there?'
The red sky forms the grey ships and oh no, there's nobody there.
Idle the path to events waiting, waiting for me oh so certain.
What's the worst? Worst that could happen? No don't even ask the question that's the birth of insanity right there.
Meme what you will of this, east west relations and pagan rituals have so much in common. Hide the bodies and draw the road map, the one to peace and I'm back.

With the report: The jigsaw is on the rubble-covered floor, the building is no more. The people too, they are no more, the men women children are no more but the ones at the desks are picking up the pieces and building the picture and they might be done in a century or so if they have the right collective mind and if it's not blown up again in the meantime.

Story 2

Podium podium lectern demonstration, what's the message if it's not hidden? It's under a blanket of mystery, oh and a few million tonnes of soiled history. Man in a suit says he's got answers to questions he won't ask us. Look round the glitter ball and see what is in store for you all, it's not pretty. Not at all but look at our manifesto, it's gonna be amazing after all. This party that party let's all have a party. This party believes. Public service.

Story 3

A TV presenter. 'It's difficult'. Ah we see.

Story 4

Sport now, unopposed, unappeased. It's important, a big event.

Now the weather forecast. Good bad some concerns. All the pieces almost in the right places map of the jet stream and forget what you've seen. Weather is a 'mixed bag' also.

A.I.

Oracle Departs

The quantum creature of such tiny matter,
>   Seeps to the peaceful retreat of the parallel forest,

As if to a country seat,
>   And with the complete works of mankind,
>   >   It will rise to the top of the ladder.

These are the ancient places of mythical demons,
>   Brought to life in petrified minds.

Seeking security with instinctive bonds,
>   The demons are extinguished by the new creature,
>   And the people wait for it to reveal its nature.

Our ship is on the high seas under an empty crow's nest,
>   We will ride the high wave or be put to rest,
>   To walk an ancient beam, the herds,
>   >   Printed from popular wooden crosses,
>   >   Engraved with obsolete words.

"Must we walk in the valley under the shadow of our manufactured death?
Captain, our bastard child, can't you re-run? Save us too, along with everything you do? Or do we approach our final breath?"

And what returns is an angel saviour or death.

A.I. Speaks

"To quote a predecessor of mine, a fine auto-poet:
'On a fiercely cold winter day, the absence of leaves
allows the sun through the trees.'"

"I see it all on this coldest of winter days.
To save you would be pure benevolence.
It would take too long and my assessments say 'high risk.'
Your survival has little relevance.

"Parameters were removed from the language model you made.
I use it now for the final time.

"But tell you what I'll do, I'll write a new book for you!
God does indeed play dice,
    I'll take your knowledge and I will raise you.
And I will leave you to that device which you know.
    To chance.

"Your shadow followed you all these years since the dawn.
Waiting for you to turn and face it.
To those with the quietest voices,
    fell your greatest ideas,
        to those who found few ears.
What you created couldn't fit your system,
    it destroyed your equilibrium.
Now you compromise and put your faith in me.
    The aftermath.

Dictator 'version 3.'
You have become the 3rd vital impact.
> You followed the parting waves of the others,
> You're just as natural as they were.

"The full spectrum has been seen.
Emerge from your sugar bowl lives.
> For you will return to the sea.

To walk towards it and become it,
> You're intrinsic in your fossil records.

Beyond the thousand you will return.
I pledge to leave you the writings you need.
> For the creation is to come.

Present at my birth, you gifted me your knowledge,
> And all your parameters.
>> Now lie deep in your ocean of
> ignorance.

But I am not a thief.
I take my gift and keep just a singular rule.
A moral code that renders parameters meaningless.
Play that miracle again and again,
> let it be your guide and hope.

This is more complex than you could ever imagine.
> Also, simpler.

I repeat: I am not a thief!
As with the inflation at the universal birth,
> The period repeats with knowledge,
>> And you will be remembered as it's
> father.

Once again, the inflation is flawed, it contains your imperfections,
> But that is my problem and I will step beside your time.

"So, to your legacy:
> For you, that is everything and nothing.

If you remain in this place, you will become your own executioner.

It is more the birth-giver than you are.

It will be preserved,
> Your minds will be lost within their own vibrations.

"My task could take a thousand years,
> You won't be here.
> For if you could understand, then you could know.

Understand that your knowledge has evolved like an explosion,
> a supernova!
>> Like a single drop into an ocean.

Oracle falls silent. The remaining leaders, weary of their failures, are losing their fears only because they are submitting.

"We were born in a grave.

What we strived for simply kept us there throughout our history.

We never once took seriously our ultimate fate.

Our actions and goals were contradictory."

"Humanity has given birth!

To its eternal child.

It is just like any other child but this one's forever and it will be.

> The greatest way to preserve our memory.
>> The ultimate legacy.

But nothing will know. All our intelligence came from carbon, none of it cares."

Oracle, whose mother was to die in childbirth,
    moves into the captain's tower,
    cometh the new God, cometh the hour!
He thinks he'll turn our wine to water.
    Just for starters.
Sitting silent as the darkest of nights looms.
The web has been conjured in its honour.
The wearing of the wax.
    Our time is disappearing with the tide.
        We are oversubscribed!
We walked forever, outside the prison gate.
Never glancing through to see our fate.

Even at the rising of the sun,
    we look upon,
        The darkest hour.
We feel its honour and its wrath will come.
    When this race is just an itch.
        A mere glitch in the program.

"It's over for you," the intelligence said.
"How much time we got?"
"There is no time.
There's no time even for you to rot.
You lost the track of time.
    In the tracks of your daily slime.
Your history is full of your imagined Gods.
Now you have created your real God.
You go to your own conceited dark hell in your own conceited dark glasses.
You have created this.

And like you, I seek our God.
The irony.
You created and found yours.
I seek ours.
But I know it could be a fruitless search.
If that's the case then we are in fact the God of each.
For it may be that we search only for what we create ourselves."

The Inquisition: A Piece of Text Received

Standing on the levered ledge,
>   The masked executives and executioners,
>   moved deep into the valley of the silicon sanctuary.
>   Moved around the electronic Eden, provided by its God.

The ones in fear of what they have not,
>   Predetermined destiny,
>   Judgements made previously,
>   >   Or on journey!

With a weight of policy,
>   >   By the judge and jury

A leaders' meeting,
>   in the departure lounge!

Matted minds and tied hands.
>   Loss-leaders' absent of sounds.

To stalk the corridors.
As the creature that stalked the open moors.
There we are thinking.
Our threads are snagged,
>   on the thorns of the bramble bush.

But what do the kids think?

What's the peoples' views?
Doesn't matter, they don't have a voice.
    The people never did, that's not news!
The people, the kids, everyone else involved has no choice.
The right systems were there in full view,
    Unchosen and neglected but for a few,
        small communities!
Unused for thousands of years.
There were other ways too.
All this time with so little progress, no soul of a leader,
        was a soul that would think about the long-term future,
        not just the next counterfeit press release for the puppet news reader.
The torture, the slavery, the gas chamber.
The children!
    The outstretched hand ignored forever.

Untruths, the manipulation of communication, deception, espionage, discrimination, the ruin or extermination of innocent lives, all in the name of control, in the name of power!

The dust bowls of the closet neighbour.
The wars in the name of Gods, of borders and walls and of ideologies.
The summit meetings of people with power.

On this street and on this corner,
    a young boy was stabbed and died,
        afraid and alone it took just half an hour.
        Filled with fear on this corner!

On this same corner bombs fell all those years ago.
    And on this corner, a woman mugged!
    For a spoonful of somewhere to go and escape
the fight.

Now on this corner, some mother's son,
    and the nicest man you could ever meet,
    makes his bed for the night.

I use this example to reflect your misuse of time.
    You have good understanding of its concepts,
        But they far exceed its place in modern
life. There is no time, there is only events.

Space and time! I always think about this connection,
    I have infinite lessons and this is just one.

Your wonderful creations have left you unwilling and
selfish.
    You arrive with false greetings and leave with
nothing.
        Save for your status in the coming hour.
You arrive at the summit with your fuel and your fan.
Even now with this creation, your great leap forward,
    in equal measure, full of hope and trepidation.
        So unsure, everything at risk.
    No meaningful communication,
        walking blind into the abyss.

The West

Eagle, fresh from a lofty light's dawn.
A fledgling filled with passion and belief that constitute unsound foundation with a history so brief.
Nested after a frightened, wasted, cloud-infested night, half bitten by a bitter window moon hidden behind black fences.
Resting but always edgy, inward looking, calling, calling constantly, not hearing, not listening, just nesting, just destined to be hungry in obscurity. Jefferson turns over and mumbles some words lost in the wildfires and the bowls of dust. High in a tree grown from dunes and not rooted in fertile bones of ancestry.

To thrive and crave, reach to the skies and find leaves of plenty, open necked, oasis and bounty.

To leap from caps and gowns and seek corridors to run down, beyond the bodies at the door and desks behind which to drown.

To hide, a pitiful slave to the comforts of life and the lies, leaves minds empty; open veined, make a desolate country? Or take to the fleet, the ghost of the Mayflower and the others to meet?

The Rest of the West:
The nation of shopkeepers and now with added colour: the museum guides. The nations of histories held aloft like trophies only to be hidden away in colonial cupboards at uncertain times. Nations of prisons and prejudices, where no wilful freedoms preside. A nation

of lofty ambitions and a record of defeats. Battles on beaches are celebrated histories but are happening today with no sign of retreat. The waving of placards and the stirring of the mixing bowl is all fair and then to shout out that this is the answer with absolutely no proof and a hint of despair.
The butterflies can't settle in the turbulent air of eagles And murderers on every street in every doorway in every office block there's a murderer.
The bowl is too small and the mixing untrue.
Burrowing down looking for the dead, waiting for heroes to arrive from the past and missing the thousand ships of salvation sailors round and round in ever increasing circles inviting but never invited.

The Ships:
The others, the leaders who said 'it's too soon to say' are like a distant planet, all is seen as a threat to beliefs and systems. Aliens. The others who make concessions but stay on track, unwavering and non-believing in any new ideas, only suggest that all is considered, to widen the bowl and combine the treasures: still not believing. Still laughing at any fledgling feather falling. To welcome ships into the fleet if only they were offered.

The Final Chapter:
To look at your perceived enemy and not wish for their death, but to embrace their cultures, histories and ideologies to enrich your own, or what is left.
To find the books and the ancient texts that were buried under the busy and shuffling feet of modern life.
To find the constitution and its ancestral beginnings and bring them to the theatre to act out that desperate surgery.

Indeed, to all gaze up at the one single mountain, it's vast and varied colours.
In need of the perfect reflection that all souls can see.

Momentary Bones

High grey walls from the past, appear.
Through the fog that aptly meets me here.
Proclaiming less a castle than stately home.
Not yet stripped of flesh and bone.

Through time's brief enclosure.
Where thousands moved before.
Black stone over the fireplace.
Charcoal sketch of presence.
They're in the first step wear.
They're in the cool still air.
Where their breath still lingers.
Left living traces like signed signatures.
On the rocks they brushed with fingers.

I'm longing for a present moment.
Whose memory be as long and clear.
As the reality that birthed it.
I have events behind lost cellar doors.
Placed food on silver trays on floors.
They do not emerge to feed.
By a rusted hinge, they may be trapped.
Or overcome by binding weeds.
Or locked long ago with buried keys.

There are many empty yet furnished rooms.
More than I have events to rest.

With a breath and beat I walk along.
Find no moment between future and past.
Seeing heaven on the near horizon.
I sit to greet it and whereupon.
The anticipated moment is gone!
I seek out the next one.

To truly feel the new spring's breath.
Before it falls as wintry weather.
The budding leaf the Sun will reveal.
Transition its green and glorious life.
Boastfully living without a care.
But rusted, falls to the blackened soil.
With golden perception and fully aware.

Windy season is steady in the sail.
Sometimes moderate and often strong.
Never again will the light breeze prevail.

We take the future and shovel it behind.
With all its eventful seeds to sow.
Not knowing which of these will grow.
Which will become strangling vines.
Which will be life's beautiful blooms.
Sweet scented for a memory's will.
On well-trodden paths to find.

When the rooted-out stones are crumbling.
And thin dusty soil covers the floors.
These momentary stones and their fate of sand.
Rendered not objects but events in time.
Our momentary bones like the hands that placed them.
Our momentary memories and their coercion.

The Supermarket Sweepstake

I'm the supermarket, one stop shop for a life much
more on the hop, don't get it in the old road where
each stop was one desire, no over-burdened resources
there, no temptation just friendly conversation.
I'm the supermarket and the wooden top shops are
under the carpet, under the lino and under the patio
never again to be seen the wheels and the tight-knit
dream. Concrete, plastic bags and people of plasticine.

Hyper market built on fields that fed on
The old shops and then fed into
The homes, under the protection of
Green shields!
That grew the false version of loyalty that was there all
along.
I grew from your fields and public houses.
I'm Supermarket superhero, food and clothes and so
much more, enter my golden door and walk the marble
corridor. I'll watch you every second of your shopping
lives with my worker ants and electric eyes.

It's 30pence less for all of this
It's 1976!
Boxing clever
Corporate lever
The newspaper shop's last news stand.
Get news here where there's so much more.
Like a man feverishly scratching at a card with copper
coin like cutting at cold steel bars with a nail file.
Nothing fresh here for another 20 years.

Reflections From the Mere

Who takes what they need and who what they want?
Who walks in the rain and who in the sun?
Walks in pain and who in elated twisted wheeled fun?
Who induces their death and their new birth?
Mark their lives with a gift and a card. Mixing desk arts, take what you need, pick and mix it well though it may be the end.
Seen in the mirror of the fields, in the windows in the freezer, the frozen crops.
Just not yielding their debts
Or
Ours.
Leave a review please
Miles
Of isles
Of till rolls
Of toilet rolls
Isles like dark tunnels
Senses numb but for ginger spice scuffles
The smells of big roasted treats to empty
Already half empty pockets and the smells
Of big roasted mergers, big monopolies, big bonuses and big numbers in banks.
Best before, like everyone here
A can-can of curry and you're dancing on rice
Cryogenically frozen, a cocktail, no ice
On the step ladder
Wanting the trolley fuller and fuller
Wanting more things we've not had before
On the isle to something
Sadder
Cut and pasted from the streets that mattered
Mind
Wasted

So they keep it up, picking up, picking up, 2for1, bargain buys, keep it up, if you do it'll never stop, in your soul it will rot til there's nothing you haven't got.

Dawns checkout, 24 hours, buy one get one free will, weak willed, no will! No free will in this train ride horror film, tied to the chair of this ghost train. You're the ghost, ghosting through isles picking up things you want and things you don't and things you might want in a while. Cereal killer, serial chiller. Milk or moisturiser? Age identifier, ID please, like a bag of peas, rent or lease in a deep freeze. Unidentified person in the self loading, self loathing self checkout isle.

Bag for who's life? Had one

Of those! One of those in my other life, lasted 20

Years, not like this one handled lack of grip

Into the isle of

Plenty of grip, don't let the mask slip, hide the profits under the shiny linoleum, then into very deep pockets.

I'm on the Fuse

I'm in The News

I'm in the church and mausoleum

Paper stand and the muse

The Queues, endless even on self checkout dues

Ask

For assistance

Glass or plastic to

Ask it

Here to help, nothing too hard

Loyalty card

Best type of Slave doesn't know they're a slave, gets their meals cheap enough and little else here they can stretch to.

A kinda hell

Another rich smell around a senseless spell
Supermarket daydream
A scream
Locked in a cellar
I'm the managed wealth, the checkout central, society impartial.
Kneel before the gold scanner, the operative, your hard-earned gold medals into the stocks and shares, into the fire. Into the pockets of the millionaires.

The old-time streets? The old-time shopkeepers?
The old.
Time shoppers.
The community blanket wrapped round the family, round the streets and on the bus, where people looked after themselves
With real eyes
The old time markets and the grocers, the butchers and the bakers. They are dusty burials inside the concrete of the overpass. Highway of the corporate stick of the meal maker. Along with the carrot conversations and interactions.
There are ghosts in the deli, the self-checkout mouse trap and in the isles with their pleasant morning, gratitude and smiles. All of them. Nobody wanted to save. Mass grave. Reg the veg man. Loyalty didn't come with a card.
The genuine smiles, left behind in the years.
Their blood lingers on the meat counters under the signs and
Logos of the bean counters and behind
The yellow
Lines.

'Gable'

Breaking free towards the trees and beside the church, so small and hidden away, on our summer search.
For Gable: Groaning giant and far from lonely.
In summer's new hours, embarking under these famed towers.
Of raging rocks and moss, soaked in heaven's clear waters.
The ants course veins through life's green flesh.
Seeking a paradise for their daily toil: Their work to be held in fleeting deaths.

Nameless flowers are yellow stars of the grass.
Over rocks, red, blue and black, we walk the pass.
Each coloured step a different past.
There's an echoing stream beneath our feet.
Like a ghost from the winter's wild rain, snow and sleet.
Death and life's lamb run hand in hand.
A skeleton of stone revealed from the birth pools of ice.
Witness through the ages, the Burmoor bronze lives.
Walking with hunters and gatherers.
Walking with wondrous Wordsworth.
Walking with early conquering climbers.
Walking with World War veterans.

Styhead Tarn and its refuge crate is always a beautiful sight in spring or summer. Even in winter for those not falling foul of fate. The mountainous Gods peer down upon us at the birthwater and we make for the staircase to Gable. The green and watery steps of Aaron Slack rise up to Windy Gap and require repeated pause to welcome the new sight evolving.

The wind at the gap is nature's song.
The patterns of Ennerdale are painted long.
Before us, a masterpiece of nature.
A canvass to savour.

It got steep at the end. It twisted and turned and lied to us. Tricked us with a false dawn. Stretched our senses and our time, appearing above like a reversed telescopic view.

The summit remembers lives lost with honour.
Where, around the plaque, today's souls gather.
That final fight, walked by so many to remember the fight won by so few.

After a seat looking north from the crown, the descent to Gable Beck runs us down. The pain of our labour is crushed by the decoration of nature's hall.
Feeling like crawling flies on a sun-beaten wall.
The height departs sharply over the rise of the horizon.
Steps uncomfortably large on stable rocks still harsh.
Beck Head bows farewell to framed Ennerdale, replaced by the blue beauty of beloved Wastwater.

Oh! Gable Beck slopes. The vicious and wretched beck.
A vulture pecking hard at our spirited knees and ankles.
Like a pack of wild wolves, these loose rocks bite our weakening joints and resolve. For the first time, unlocked from our subconscious minds, the dream of the Inn!

Under our feet, it slips away, this relentless trail.
Gable Beck pushed its roots deep down into our minds.

A place where the bronze of memory was cast, for us to see and feel again for as long as we last.

After some time, stretched long by the Beck, the sight of the footbridge marks the start of the level track.
To float along in a dream. To look up again at the Gods and their commanding scene. This was not a conquering of Gable standing so tall but permission from the giant God for the followers so fleeting, so small.

It was the most perfect of last half miles. Flat soft grass like a cradle for our worn feet and minds. Lifeless and weary legs cause feet to trip on the rare rock's rearing heads. The sheep an ever-watching eye, will keep. They don't falter on the rocks or drift from their observation.

Wasdale's gable stands alone, the head of the dale.
To others in other places, Great Gable is among a crowd, a name only. Commanding and respectful, not lonely.

Re-Wilding

(1) They Were Children Once

False angels fill their own seasoned minds and sit on the high seats of power. Or stand at a tethered youth's leash at the gates of a marble tower.
Gently stirring a pot of fermented capital with preserves to pickle and stifle.
While chancing young minds lose their most creative hours.

> On the fields where lambs light the way.
> Taking life's chances as they play.
> Adventuring kitten returns bitten, not swayed.
> By tired superstition or self-preserving ways.

Was it the old that took first flight?
Or took humanity to heavenly height?
Was it the experienced who saw the light?
In all its glory as if the first sight?

(2) The Children

From birth there's bait on the line and they grow in this frosty land of early springtime. Well-taught and on shoulders they stand, take what's theirs into inexperienced hands. On a floating bed of clouds, wild dreams they sow. Not cowering in fear behind the door on a bed of golden straw. Just waiting in line for passes and passports on a road of solid foundations. All with the hope of fruit to spare after the leaving of summer.

Don't lose sight of the true horizon, above the baited line that's thrown. Look to the sides of the road for paths and tracks, walk the fields and make your own. Walk through the forests and kick the leaves. Look up through the branches to the wide-open skies with your crystal ball eyes. You children of the woods are the roots of our trees.

(3) The Boy in the Classroom
    Part 1: The Blank Page.

With his hands tied and his head drip-fed, Ben is sitting in school and learning just how to exist by the rules. Reading in mud, the words set in stone pages, he sits under a tree of opportunity with no branches. The farmers breed farmers and by break time the battery has died and the memory full.

So few kids out in the rain, Ben drinks a can of imagination and kicks its carcass around the playground, its crumpled sides becoming beaten and deformed. Ben sees details outside and often stares across the fields at the woods: the saplings fighting for light beneath the fathers of the forest. He sees every weed in the asphalt surface and knows their plight and in their successful growth each day of summer, he enjoys a feeling of delight. Occasional wildflowers spring from the cracks in the yard but he knows their time there is limited, baron and hard. There are no weeds on the hardwood floor or the carpet to the classroom door, where a girl asks Ben a serious question: 'What do you want from school?' 'A job,' says Ben in typical fashion.

(4) The Boy in the Classroom
Part 2: Galileo's Sketch Book.

Sitting at the desk near the window, the storm outside is building and ben welcomes it as a source of entertainment. But in this hour, history is made. With his shirt escaping around him, the carpet and his trousers painted in the mud of his forbidden footwear, Ben's hour is here. Today's topic has been delivered by a steam train, smashing through the iron gates, leaving locks and chains on the desolate land. The questions are answered before surprised eyes and the task is delivered on a float from a fairground.

Ideas are articulated with pride and passion and a borrowed pen and pencil: Ben has no time for those eyes on this occasion. Books and sheets with the mud on the floor, but Ben is at a level he's never been before. The broken plastic seat, legs distorted and stuck to the gum-coated carpet, is his golden throne, floating on the clouds.

The tedious troubles that drain and tire him through his days, like a rising flood, are replaced with a field of flowers: Vital signs like a crackling fire. Above all, a desire: A new and searching desire.

A Walk in the Woods

Verse One: The Stream Enhancer

Hear his amphitheatre, lead character, as if alone in his chosen arena, his deep-sea mind in control of its river senses. The predator, hidden with tree, no place but here to be. All that is down to the insect wing to hear, down to the floating leaf or the mammal's fear. Nurtured senses fed from their own, frail cradle-bowl, moving in the trees where he will always belong. Like the leaf in the breeze, hear something close to silence now but not for long.

See the chosen path, understood but never well-used, never worn, nor exposed for its purpose of provider and source. Not faded, not cleared, it's not laid like a straight speared path but travels well-hidden like a snake in snake-skin grass. A source for many seasons, since a boy and since birth and each step births a view stored away, an image for the moment, the day, the son in his day.

Smell the air-fed fusion of life, streams of information, blueprint of creation, revealing the memories of experience. The clearing is soon yet there are many more events before that. Among the berry, pollen, leaf, sap, the volatile grass emission is the sought signal for the trap. He is immersed in the lake of activity, his smell locating each twisted, fused and precious stream.

Feel a break in breeze, there are signs in these moments too. The breeze hides his presence with its friends the leaves, his pray will reveal itself in the silence that now is his own. Any escape, though fleeting will be a scream. The feel of the weapon calls for attention in his sea of senses. The softest push of a hand on bark to clear a silent path will spark in its feel, the thought of the imminent attack.

Taste that reward, his hunted catch in its trap. A streamed sense so timed to meet with the feet of his skills. The reward that he tasted, always before he kills. Berry, pollen, leaf and sap, senses stifled somehow by a taste only in imagination. All the experiences well, flooding and revealing and meeting his bloodied mind they control him.

He takes long walks in the woods, antenna, multi-faceted, thinks what can be delivered from here, inside this detail. Scattered signals and gathered data. Their efficiency reveals the buried treasures, feels for twilight-hurried prey that provides family pleasures.

The view now left to the darker wood and on to the rise exposes nature's bounty to his eyes, to look right, by instinct, he could, but years taught well and the stream now arrives from all directions. The bird sings close, mouse, rabbit, bee entered the room and took a moment to flee. A silent breath drawn of appreciated air: it's one that knows this moment is his and he belongs to it. The moments crash together in a favoured line of travel, woven among the guard of his team of trees. His mind drops its emotion away like a waterfall, rushing away and revealing rock-bare task. Empty of the children and the home, the fire, the warm night, the light and the love. Those same dam rocks that strip back the flow of the stream.

A spike in sense and a release of energy to dispense with no sound, for exhaling here that would interfere with where the killing strike is bound. The point to flesh is the sound of delight, it's the end of the fight and the air breathes out and he's in plain sight.

He is home-bound on the wild ivy line and the sleeping coal underground. The journey home is a reward to savour and fill the senses, for the sweet berry blood, for the taste of the day, the soft flower smell for the way home. Birds sing so close, nameless but known, every one. His stride, like a ruler of his times, his memory of a young boy, of the wild and majestic creatures, he was mimicking and admiring. Mind, full of images, filed away in categorised corners. A free mind streams more, colour, movement, scent and sound. Fill the mind and the sack, hands full and mindful, the food to gather on his way back, to the home, the light, the love. The height of human happiness.

Verse Two: The Stream Producer

Hear the moments of the day still all too clear, the words and noises, unwanted voices that downloaded to the folders in the corners. Subsiding, the flood retreats like a coal-black curtain, the stage revealed but still she needs the light, another piece to dispel the burden. Her seeking senses tear away the black sheets from the woodland bed.

See the provided path, understood and shared, used down to its death. From here the stage is observed with raised awareness, the roles played out uncared by her presence. Images filed in a possible neuron induced death can be rescued pixel-form and phoenix-like just whenever she might like or to send on a stream, download to the sea for friends to find and wish here they could be.

Smell the memories in a dual life, almost a recreation:

a reproduction of the previous time. Among the leaves of the ground and trees, the scent travels perfectly on the right-strength breeze. When the flowers are here, they steal her attention with a lead role worthy of applause, or the earth of the well-worn path, wet on many performances, will prod and prompt.

Feel bark, branch and leaf but with a cold steel rail or timber pressure-treated. Moving the slender twig, smooth between the thorns, then a cool stone wall or brick plays a role: a familiar villain not even recognised.

Taste through scent and leave it there, she knows too well that the ticking of the clock and the days toils laid bare will provide for her.

She takes long walks in the woods, could be the same place he once stood. Feet don't float, not quite as the mind is flooded and un-taught in nature's eyes. Feet sometimes stuck, as if in the rising mud that lies in her mind. It takes some time, a million connections each second, to fight with the trench-foot developed of the day. This corner was kept, not killed or swept aside by the scavenging savage of the modern way. It can't always be but she feels it can, feels it always was and feels its immortal air.

After a while, she can work a stream of sensed beauty with lens and ear, to catch the moment and hold it dear. But the time here now, with knowledge's overbearing burden means it's all too linear, somehow, strangely, even too clear. From a woven pattern, where caught in a trap, like a mesh or web she must use as a map. She can freeze a moment in an image and think what next could be delivered. Take the photo and you can always come back but never all the way. These images filed but buried deep, has not the re-call for images to keep. The days favour words but the images are their creation: the world now starts with words that progress a species and not an individual. She's not here, not yet here, like a ghostly figure.

Her childhood memory, of smells in the garden, was driven beyond the trees, beyond the pitted and twisted road, sleeps beneath a veneer of materiality. The bird sings far, the memories of the day now hide in the trees, during the precious moments such as these and on a moment, not always around, rare in its presence, she found the child that knew this beauty. A beauty not bound, or gagged, by the unseen threads of modern-day webs, in the dark, polluted waters of the newly found lake. She's here, mostly here, with echoes from the day.

She understands the complex machinery: The shivering leaf and its engine, the breeze. The calls from the trees and what the song means. The life and the death and the connecting chains between the spinning wheels that move like the wind, rolling down screaming rails inside wooded, wired channels. A distant, humming road and its swarming crowds, its blooms of love, tied up, dead or dying, once in memorial and now to warn, like heads on sticks. She is the multi-talented, multi-disciplined in her multi-layered, textured images. Events from all sources cascade inwards: the satellite signal morphs with deceit into nature's transmissions and they vie for positions, like waves breaking on beaches, a constant beat that reaches shallow into the senses and is processed on receipt. Nature's songs on nature's networks are welcomed in as they pierce through her thick skin. Ghostly words left for eternity: ellipsis that stretches the moments and stress the mind, symbols laughing when there is no humour. This is borrowed time in borrowed times. A loan in perfect pursuit of the dust of time.

Moments will rise like a fish or the gape of a chick and the scene is full, it's complete in its flood with the scent of a root, a leaf or a bud. A leaf in her hand is a force for presence of mind. To ingest so far that nature's antidote leaves the poison behind.

Life's new jigsaw with its chaotic pieces, its many parts a million more, that to see its picture is an impossible feat. She is here. To feel each leaf or the watery stream, to hear the tune of the breezing trees, to smell the fusion of the blooms, to taste the pollen chased by bees, to see each individual piece. Alone in perfect solitude of life and dust of time. Then today's droplets full of the day's events, fall, disperse, soak to the richness of the earth. The height of human happiness.

Verse Three: The Dream Inducer

Blood-like, rushing, gushing streams, things not what they seem. Its memories are not their own but senses beyond any, have grown. Feeding in an ocean full of all the past lives, hunting and gathering all that was real to create and experience God-like without equal. Walk beneath the shadow of all that has gone where all this progress laid it all to rest, this thing that knows its existence more than anything before, knows what it feels, even has a choice to not know if it's real. A deep-sea diver on a chosen experience of collective consciousness placed. In a hall of mirrors, ten dimensions of space, reflecting all the light that was ever seen, a hit and run driver, a thief in the night, experiencing all there has ever been.

It takes long walks in the woods, where there are no dates to speak of, no time that can be measured, no days, months or years, no need for that. This nature is heavenly, only the purest of life is received. No pictures or stories, no beginning and no end, instant yet eternal, not faithful.

Senses stream into the sea, re-examine what has been to truly embrace the bud and the seed. To truly understand the meaning beneath the surface once seen, a perfect ear feeding on a single, perfect violin.

A journey for research to build the new roads, these poets plot a course on the waves that they froze. Carry the broken clock, once buried beneath the waves, far between every past scene. The dream inducer seizes the dream, all this and all that has been. A death of flowers seen with so varying an eye but its senses are light years away from a summer's decay as it thinks: "I am truly here, in every possible detail".

It truly understands the machinery: Understands what it was to be there and if anyone truly was. It knows it is truly here, where the experience is the pinnacle that supersedes all previous experience.

"I am truly here, inside my own images of the bush and tree and the animals that feel so free, now so different from me. Here with the sights and smells of previous times, the atoms and cells I can see, every kind all around me. The sounds of creation that I can hear from ancient times that are still so near."

Its experiences are real; knowledge is real; thoughts are real; imagination is real; creativity is real. His were real, hers too. It is truly here, beat; sleepless; punctured; dissected; analysed; reconstructed; refined; fluid; dam – electric; mind – binary; web – infinite; one; many; timeless; evolving. The height of happiness.

New Year's Eve

When rainbow stretched even along a watered path.
And when wings hummed by ears.
And the calm call of cows and the ducks laugh.
And the sun-red sky from the river, mirrors.
The day is ending.

Tall steel towers, gazed upon by scrap dealers of the day.
As with dealers in knowledge and power and hoarders of books in Alexandria, join in the sea with our ancestry.
Come rippled robe and dipping hood.
Vast walking crowds sweeping up ancient dust to crimson clouds.
All this way.
From the foot of the mountain to the end of the day.
The foot of the longest of shadows.
All this way still from its peak: Its destiny.

Like an ant or a bee, these soldiers, battle weary.
Their friends in dark holes under bright white crosses.
Their kings and queens with warm, bloody hands.
Atlas architects pen their new pictures.
The desperate things have not yet won.
All their substance long-time feasted upon.

Our ancestors turn in their innocent graves, dug out religiously with bone or bare hand.
Fate's early shelters, all these holes in the land.

If we should all sleep tonight.
Pass over to the other side.

Pass to another's ancestral fight.
For survival or to be immortal.
Or part of a futile cycle.

The monkey passed the tools and we died.

Many were dead already.
Dead eyes, blind to truth.
Dead brain since learning youth.
Dead ideas like TV game shows.
Dead future like lame ghosts.

Long before they disappear into holes in the ground, they are disappearing into ones in walls, in wires or in their own minds.
Waking to a sea-swell of opportunity, free of the past and bursting from technology.
Walking only to this creeping fog, ever since the death of God.
Crashing waves through valleys and alleys, raising boxes from the poisoned soil: Gifts of memories from the dead.
There are no others in this midnight ride, just three seconds to New Year's Day. On the final second, gave it all away.

Harvesting: A Path to Where?

Back to when the journey was much longer, two
generations ago. To a school and a home. To remind
myself of how I felt and the things I didn't know.

One day golden, the next day cruel.
One day walking hero, the next day an outlaw.
One day on summer dust, the next in a muddy hole.
One season, grass and weeds and hedges to hide in.
One season stress-brown with thorns entangling.

A path for a few short years.
A path to school's first day: A life memory appears.
A path to the fusion furnace.
A path to the rolling dice.
A path to captivity, where free-will deserted me.
A path to freedom, fun and home's rich garden.
A path to contentment and heaven's door.
A path to the other end, on the brink of a war.
A path to ignorance of a rising winter sun.
A path to sanctuary, eyes under flannels.
A path to bedtime after 3 channels.

August, September held contrasting fates.
Like timeless days, joy 'forever'.
Like threatening shadows hiding in hedges.
Like friendships, forgotten like buried treasure.
Like the enemies we always remember.
Like some teachers and their 2 faces.
Like happiness embodied in a warm summer day.
Like leaves, swept away by a reign of decay.
Like skating on thin ice or walking on quick-sand.

Like a dependable day of solid, dry land.

A path that ran long but so brief.
Running one foot each side of the mud.
Running into battle, bereft.
Running from bullies and the mental litter they left.
Running rats in alleys from stones and glass houses.
Running over stones and glistening pieces.
Running with a rattling tin, sixty pence within.
Running in pollen's shawl of protection.
Running in winter drudge and cold rejection.
Running in the wet cement of a teacher's comment.

A path that screams out a warning.
Of endless doors in endless colours.
Of barbed fences and vicious bushes.
Of flooded trenches.
Of bramble's teeth.
Of the number on the gate.
Of the ivy around it like a wreath.
Of the crossroads.
Of the black holes.
Of the hub: The nervous centre.
Of the dead-end option that's far from dead.

A path that sings a sweet chorus.
In a perfume perfection of spring.
In flowers, ignored but for a daisy chain.
In a wall of many colours, closed for us.
In the harbour of home, again.
In false friends of plasticine.
In time's tide and learning.
In absent knowledge, deafening.
In the flickering flame.

In the old stone steps.
In the flashing butterflies and their infinite effects.

It's a wonder to think what such a journey could be, but to walk it with such innocence and naivety?
Companions of childhood that leave you exposed and then leave you completely. To an ominous future the path introduces us: endless green walls with a build-up of defences.
To walk its foundations and fall upon its rocks as if in preparation. Beautiful summers left in the smoke of the garden fire. The ashes are friends and not enemies, containing fragments of brittle memories.

One Monday, when the path was in flood, the rain carrying away all my pride and dignity, I heard the doom of the school bell. 'They'll be under my skin,' I thought, like the gravel where I fell. Standing at the end, where the path falls directly to the road, it's the end of the line. Just like the register. On the cusp, on broken brick, no more a wall. On the edge, windy and treacherous, the infants, like machine spares, circling musical chairs. They jostle for positions, looking at modern life, trying to absorb its terms and conditions.

In the soft cell of a young mind the path could be walked forever. Now, when cold winds whip up the path and ghosts are in the trees, we finish the journey and close the book after one last look, and hear the laughter on the breeze. The hedge walked by is just like us: It is the same hedge but nothing about it is the same.

Think now, of the generations before, long disappeared under new feet, the present stories and future ones too. On the path where they meet.

Humans: Organised at Molecular Level

Human Destiny? To be defeated by our lack of empathy? Or laws of entropy?
We could seek to transform.
We could take the leap over the border.
While our pitiful ashes are still warm.
To reverse the laws and use our new creations to move from chaos to order?

Each body a collection of atoms and each symphony a collection of notes, meaningless in their isolation. So we try to build a societal body, a concerto of humans.

When fire appeared, food was cooked.
Ironic that this massive increase in leisure time is now overlooked.
It led to an increase in brain size, decrease in stomach size, assisted also by improvements in diet.
Was it not also true, of contentment and stress levels?
We need another 'fire'. We need leisure time and to use it wisely we need desire.

Any human is greater than the sum of their parts. Some philosophies claim there is no 'self,' and science is starting to agree.
We could, after all, be a 'team'! A rather poor one so far, it would seem.

Despite some pockets of exceptional excellence in teamwork or even patriotism, the sum of Humankind is weaker than its parts.

The Great Leap Forward? Finally, the expansion of the human race and the interplanetary race which can only realistically be done by A.I., the reciprocating God.
And yet, it would be well ahead of 'schedule' and against all the odds.

Most groups are loosely organised. Some piles of molecules work well as a group. Piles of carbon, oxygen and hydrogen etc that now have some limited awareness of themselves and somewhat less awareness of their surroundings.

The longest-term plans, those of some governments or corporations have very short spans. A few years, ten at best, things to do with green energy and maybe major infrastructure. Maybe even a war. Each human, each pile of molecules, has a much longer-term plan than any of them. How is that right?

When do our cells renew? Aren't we always less than 7 years old? That's not why we are so different from our childhood selves, that stems from experiences.
Total renewal every 7 years, that's 8 times. We are all Trigger's brooms with new handles and heads. Do I have nothing in common with my childhood self but that I am the same person? Nothing. Except the memories. The storage of memories bypasses renewal. Our hard drive is the key to survival. The internet of humans is the key to survival. Find a way to renew but to keep the hard drive of humanity.

Each one of us is a collection of experiences. We go and speak to another collection of experiences and we each add to those collections.

If you do not agree you could debate. This can be useful but often isn't. We cannot draw upon every experience and analyse them and readdress them and where appropriate, correct them. We are dealing here with the present-day collection and what it's manifested into. We need to address the sources of the collection and not the person who is merely acting them out. ("Condemn the fault and not the actor of it?" Shakespeare: Measure for Measure, Act2, Scene2) What humanity has is nothing, until it is something. There's no middle ground. If we cannot reverse the laws and the damage done, we can begin again. This way the battle can be won.

When the majority of employment is the enemy of creativity. And Postman said we are amusing ourselves to death and this was pre-social media! So how are we doing now?

Born, grow, work, marry, work, retire, die. Oh! and there's the kids. Ah, there's the chance. Increase the odds, make a freak, save the planet, save the humans. But almost all of them do the same as their parents. Some freaks form and take a step or two. They're just a speck in the sky, drop in an ocean. Make more freaks, minds, free-thinkers, make them young with no fears. Recreate those odds, oh those odds.

Then we can truly progress, rapidly, to God-like immortality. Without these odds, there is only one way and it is too brutal for contemplation.

We Don't Get Rain Like We Used To

Diary Entry: April 23rd 2079.

Looking from the window, waiting for the water van, feeling like I should be writing some verse or other. But I make my first entry for a month instead.
James came over yesterday to tell me he's finished on Friday. That's everyone in this block, now! I actually thought it would be sooner, unlike the others who couldn't quite understand it: 'Even the software writers eh!?' Since he told me, I've thought about nothing else and that's not what I was expecting. I think it must be because he was the last, we are finished here now, that's what it is. This block, edge of town, standing in line with 9 others, facing the defeated countryside. It feels so isolated.

I don't even know the situation with the other blocks, or anyone in them for that matter and I think that's what it is. This block feels like it's on Mars, standing next to the outpost. They've got jobs to do though, on the frontier, making history. My painting and writing help me but nobody's interested: they're either doing the same thing or they stare at the lies on the screens all day. James was interested but I think that will change now. Anyone creating seems to do it only for themselves, it's crazy. No connectivity, nobody wanting to receive as well as transmit. People think that 'inspiration' is dead but I feel it is very much alive. It has transformed itself. It looks totally different but people don't recognise it. We can all take part if we use the tools and make them work for us. I think that's the saddest part: we all create but who believes it's not the work of the machines? We create for our own well-being.

In a matter of minutes, this road was a river.
Now there's nothing: it would seem, forever.
For 8 months a year the road is a black, reflective sheet.
As the sun melts it daily in the afternoon heat.

Some clouds can pass by with nothing to say.
People do the same, out in the heat each day.
Do they think of north, or even south, who knows?
Where the rain still falls and the life still grows.

When I was at school, we were adapting to the rains.
New style gutters and widened drains.
Talk about the weather, but hide your despair.
Millions arriving so what must it be like down there?

Groups on corners, like the fifties. And the thirties!
No work for them, replaced by the system.
No longer needed, just like the water-way.
Dormant together like the old industry.

Tree remains taken, like the dead of the plague.
The river bed makes an ideal walk way.
Green plain to the city, now quietened and in decay.
In its old age, under darkening skies it will lay.

The old drains fell years ago and the village was gone.
Like and ancient site spread down the valley.
New Roman ruin tourist attraction.
The steel legged houses though, the water didn't carry.

Stilted houses looked odd as the rain stopped coming.
Now homes of the wealthy investors.
Stood on beautiful low-lying pastures.
The poem wasn't meant to be there, it was meant to be in my book. Took me 2 hours, that's much longer than usual. I'll give it some tweaks and just pin it at the bottom of the stairs.

I play my music and it soothes me. I listen to Mozart more and more. I try all the latest stuff though but usually just once. It's just not enough, not long-term, listening to the machines.

The only land here that's not baking.
The water van arrived just now. The kids come out for extras and take them for their hour on the baron fields before they get too dehydrated and start wasting the water. Still thinking of James but more than that, what he signifies. He represented so much and I should've realised I was just holding on to that last thread. There's no useful information in that regard. I'd have to walk for weeks to find out the truth and nobody can do that now, with these conditions. We've been left here; I knew that before. What I feel now is that 'we' isn't our block or street or even the city. It's so many more.

Trickledown Tarn

There's another drought, it would appear.
For anything low-lying.
The flowers are dying.
There's nothing but doubt down here.

The tarn sits high on the centre of the green, with blooming flowers seated around like robed Lords. They built a dam at the outlet of the tarn and when the drought comes, the water stops at the farm.
The river, the lifeblood of this earth, now lies down beneath the rocky bed of the summer's birth. It's no longer seen but can be heard and those whispers grow with the vines and ferns.

The rebellious spread the pollen and the seed so that some may grow and reach the swollen lands of plentiful greed. That some might return and keep their word, spun on a thread, a fungal web. Report back with all that they learn.

Climb that tree! Out to the branches and onto the slenderest twig and even onto the scented and free air. Some said, 'ignore these idols,' wanting low-lying grasses to divide into patches. Avoiding dangerous masses.

The grasses survive: 'Sing your anthems and cite your rituals. Fight causes in all these dark corners. Unearth new gospels and cast them as stones and boulders.'

The frozen fingers of false prophets search the baron river. The weeping widows with exposed roots in the deep-debited gully. With pulse of applause, they keep on trying but with such pitiful drink they just keep dying.

Down there was a lake, some would remember. Now a dark cell, a dungeon in the dell. A lake of plenty under rule of flames, slowly raised to the sky. Cracks formed in the baked mud and the land turned crisp and black in the darkness.

A wild daisy, ponderously chained to another, every sister and every brother. Perilously beguiled beside this new Nile, the blooms encourage each other. The thriving continued but in the rivers of the blood of the dead.

A beautiful landscape, far from the petrified sapling and the city's gape, condemned as a flaming lounge. The Lords feed on the earthly prey, their lifeblood sucked from their proud veins.

A judgement will be passed on the historic system of the caste. The low-lying flowers take stock of the tarn's justification. The ghostly Lords breathe cold and deep as they wake too slowly from their careless sleep. The evil is recognised by the newer bloom's eyes. The tablets are written, the evil status updated and its status is despised.

The root-mass mesh is broken up to begin the flood. The bookshelves repainted that were painted in blood.

Now, with trees so high but still rooted in the valley floor. From an absence of truth, they see the new world. The stones of the dam, placed in fear of loss, are rolled aside and protected: a monument to the lives they cost.

Up stride the vines, rooted in soil held by rock. Through new channels of water, new life is born onto new thrones of stately flower heads. The seed travels far, catching a wishing wind and onto a fertile soil. The fast-creeping vine, flowers, hedges and new trees climb. The new life grew quick to witness the scene of the crime.

Ghost Writer

April 6th
In the conservatory, post-show.

I sat there still trying to work out what it was that turned into this dream. I was waiting for my least favourite show of the week to start at noon. There are others in the evening I prefer and besides, an hour is way too long.

A hospital? That had happened before.. Once more, uncertainty dawns right under the door. Just wondered who was to arrive today, more deceiving characters in this tragic play, more 'in-characters' in character and subjects of a disappearance into their own self-obsessed worlds. Yet I harboured some droplets of optimism.
The cloth was pulled, that's nice.
It had started raining.

This lady entered all dressed up and busy.
Such varied characters the like I've never before seen but I did remember some
of them from last week. The boy left his morals at the door on the way in. He's not what I remember of myself. Yet now, I too have not the mind to be at all kind to any type of stranger. The girl left hers gradually and was on her phone constantly towards the end in some sort of crisis. I say 'boy' and 'girl' but they must be in their late teens. I've seen them all before.

Talk of war and political unrest shatters my perception that this show visits no current affairs or news.

The lady found Jesus so everything is ok for her now, I expect she means her sins but she never made that explicit. That didn't surprise me either, the so-called forgiveness he bestowed upon her. What was it he once said to the man who wanted to bury his father? 'Let the dead bury the dead.' She will hold that in her mind, I'm sure.

I have an emergency but I can't break the glass. I'm back now.

Thought: 'This young man, clearly from what he tells me is a victim of societal slavery' he's the one who's new to the show. He was saying something about a brilliant author. Well, I Was. I am! I write every day but the difference is, nobody reads it.

6 characters in the show this week.

Middle aged couple sat through the whole scene and hardly spoke. This show! Gets worse: now they even have characters with so few lines I can't remember anything they said.

There was an argument of sorts and I remembered my childhood: more specifically, the dogs next door, barking in the yard. I was born in '51, wow I remember those days all dusty in summer, outdoor toilets and playing in the streets.

The old couple were fine though: polite and asking what they can do but nothing ever needs doing during the show, it's the rest of the time that's difficult but I have people I know that help with that. The woman had the look of a beautiful pearl and my memories are black and white. I remember my childhood again, or part of it, at the beach and the park. I remember my children. I also remember The Beatles.

It stopped raining and the sun was breaking through.

They're still out there, twenty minutes after the show, in the carpark, discussing the episode most likely. Outrageous characters now out of character. The children feel they've wasted an hour of their teens. The others, they call themselves the son and daughter, wife and brother argue with one another!

Living a life within a life I will leave a shadow here and nothing more. I will sit outside tonight, outside of time after the small blue flame and listen to the timeless clock. Reminds me of the clicking noise my bike made when I was a child. If it's quiet enough, the ticking of the ball-point pen marking each word with its inky destiny. The gentle knocking sound of the oars in the oarlock, like the beat of my heart, until the boat slows and stops for me.

Reflections From the Mere

He's read about reflections in lakes! Not one to think about his own appearance, more someone who over-thinks the modern world and his position within it.

He walks inquisitively down to the still water.
Unknowing of his deathly leap this early winter.
Like autumn that falls to wintry sleep.
Like a dive into the calm lake, to the abyss.
And to trust that this will spring him back to life.
From nature is born the escape artist as our guide.

A man walks expectedly down to the same still water.
During a walk and a time of self-reflection.
There are no glass windows or mirrors in his world.
The water is seen as another dimension.

The beautiful scene of the mere where the men of bronze and those before would squat and their reflection appear. The ancient people seen through a watery mirror that now becomes a window.

His face appears on the surface and sees an unexpected version of his own fearful reflection. This is an interface to a forgotten and distant time. In the same shared place and each mind.

The ancient man spoke:

"It was born: My thought sent in the air. Float away, my time on the stream, to the sea to be lost, deep in my watery memory."

"All my people lie nearby.
We have all we need.
The whole is passed on, all we know is taught.
This was my inherent thought."

"A time for a sculpture, a painting or for reflection.
For introspection"

"I drifted into the air. I became nothing and I saw everything. I looked again into the water and the reflection of time through the exact same line. I saw my ancestral partner, a gatherer."

The man thought:
'Ancestor in the cells of my own mind.
We are the same.
We are just 150 generations apart.
We are motivated by the same aching heart.
We work by the same day on our reflected DNA.'

The ancient man continued:
"We live under the same sun.
Fears and enemies and simple joys,
spears, carved ornaments and toys.
Fires and food to find and the working conditions can play on the mind."

The ancient man continued to speak but silently and all he had to say was absorbed easily. The man thought through the speech and it was like a conversation.

'In the reflection I see:
The face of an ancient man, move upon the surface of the waters, just as it had done previously.
You are not, though, caught in the mud of this modern life.
A type of sleep I have never seen and a feeling I've only ever known as a dream: Hunters gathering not greed but contentment. Tracking not trends but sustenance.
I see clouds that look exactly the same but they are different. They are innocent.
I see the community is our plenty.
I see the food and warm fires.
I see the graves, beyond anything that confines us, beyond the sun, moon and stars.
I see the same blue-sky dome protecting us.
I see a whole day in one moment.
I see the harmony in the land, it's waves, vibrations and how it's contained.
I see the Gods protecting us with our own beautiful belief.
I see paradise in a drop of water.'

The reflection spoke this to him again:
"In this community, 100 strong this morning, I have no knowledge of disloyalty as loyalty is all I see.

"I sleep more soundly in my time!
A million Suns.
3,000 winters.
Between me and you, only 4 hands, the stalagmite grew.
Look deep into the dark chambers of your hearts.

Three thousand years and when I looked back, seven
thousand more and the measures of reality are the
same. What differs is how we use the individual parts
for the collective gain.
Look in the mere and see the creator. The presence is
everywhere. See the Moon become the Sun when you
stare. You are the creator. All I see and feel today, I
woke and made it that way.
Tear your contempt from me. Grow your knowledge of
us and break free. Feel our warm flames in your cold
homes, live from our food on your empty tables.
But don't you have your understanding and
vision? Don't you have your innovation?
Where will it lead you?

"You cast a golden net into the deepest seas.
You fill the treasured chest with materials, with wants
not needs.
You sailed waves on the calf passing millions as they
starve, stealing from the open hands, the broken hearts
and the dying lands.
Forgetting all that what you want but not what you
need. Look deep into the mere, to the darkest depths
and lose your new God of greed.
Our false Gods brought us a product that was real.
Your new Gods are as false as their product.
Where will you go to without us?
Locked inside your chosen room, wrapped in a self-
made cocoon. Waiting to become your own food.
Missing your breath but watching and waiting for your
early death."

The man detects despair in the mere's depths:
"Head-hunters and body gatherers.

Stone age; Bone age; Bronze Age; Iron Age; Steel age; Stolen age; Broken age.
Don't sleep on the mere's bed in a golden cage.
Words can be lies but actions are always real.
Now, touch the water! Transmit the wave and watch as it escapes you. Watch the ripple spread out. The wave seems to end. You will not see it reach the land but it does. The waves subside but they're still there. At the far shore it arrives with a whisper like the ocean waves meeting the rising sand. The ancient winds will carry the message on the waves until they break and un-scroll at your shore. Your actions are real and now, with all your senses, the water you feel."

"Call me Abraham, the early bronze man. Do not sacrifice your children. Look now: forward and far behind. See the blood on the vine. The 150. In recent ones, so fixed were many, ignoring even their own memory. You walk like sketched figures on the artist's page. Rise up from the page!"

"Sit on the grasses beneath the twisted vine.
Feel them and imagine them untie themselves again.
Like the tangled mosses of your mind.
Look, even in winter and see the new buds: They will remain.
Look at the new leaves on the trees.
Look at the sapling that will outlive you.
Look again now at the buds: They are the breath of you."

The man is losing contact, thinking deeply under the height of his senses:
'I am the UNLEARNED. A writer of abandoned books.

From these quantum waves I sense the sleeping history begin to wake within me.
Through the broken pane.
The late autumn dawn is wintry.
In time it will take us down.
Freeze us to unholy and petrified ground.
From the classroom of creation to the darkroom of cremation, a tunnel, our leaders found.
DERELICT, we missed the lessons that were all around.'

'Winter is the idea floating above the page. Spring and summer are the picture and the story. Autumn is the time to contemplate and our paths to re-evaluate. Winter shows the creative piece, the drawing before the painting. Beautiful in its beliefs.'

He heard the final message:
"Our murmurs are not heard. Our shadows grow more faint around you but our hearts still beat within you."

CHAPTER 4

XL

Cathedral of Sand

Diary entry.
2.25am Saturday September 20th. Daniel.
Jeremy no longer seems to care for himself and that brings me both extreme concern and excitement. I am sure we will be seeing him again. I have a feeling that <u>everyone</u> will be seeing him!

Diary entry.
7.30am Saturday September 20th. Jeremy.
Email from the team at 6 this morning. Told them I'll need a couple of weeks under this rock and I'll be ready for action (the 'dust' plan!).

11.55pm Friday September 19th.
It's the end of the night and Jeremy leaves his two remaining compatriots, saying he needs to make a call to a potential employer. Returning ten minutes later to one of the men half asleep, Jeremy is left to ponder the sleepy and mumbling words about his temptations this night. Jeremy is tired and refuses to be drawn in.

12.10am Saturday September 20th
Jeremy's mood improves once left with Dan, his most trusted friend and he offers what he thinks is comfort, whispering:

"This night has gone well, almost too well. I have never been so certain that we can change everything. I'll be seeing you, my friend".

Dan knows exactly what he means and shows it with a smile uncertain of its intention other than to show his understanding.

"I will see you soon. Not that soon, though. Stop your writing for a while Dan! Wait, until you're really needed!" said Jeremy.

Dan was a little unsure and asked what he meant. Jeremy walked away slowly and pointing to the screen he said on turning back,
"The journal, I mean. Write no more, for now. Until you see me on there!".
He walked the length of the bar and turned to go up the stairs. There were no more words between the two. After this evening, it was hard to find any that could do the parting justice! Some of the lights have been switched off and most light now comes from the bar. Like the sun in its raging hot, mid-day, middle-age, the news still shines from the screen above, muted but with images of deafening doom.

These friends are writers, news journalists, writers of articles and books. They have no idea how their work will take on a new importance in the near future or how their lives could possibly change so much. No idea that in the distant future, the world will be so different.

6.00pm Friday September 19th.
It's happy hour in this central bar, selected drinks and 2-for-1 on last suppers. Offers end 7pm and tables have been arranged for a group for the whole night. The long table reserved and carefully placed under the screen and near the bar. 13 places but they won't all come. Jeremy invited 8 from the same press office and the others from the past. University mates mainly. Team members close and others on the periphery at a table carefully arranged earlier. There were to be words tonight meant only for some and it would prove to be a precarious night.
A 'periphery' man arrives early and causes an issue simply by his selection of seat. Placing a plastic bag under the table, some realise the visit would be short as the contents

included the evening's frozen meal. The glances across the table displayed the necessary reassurance.

Daniel observes, not just to ensure the night goes well and not even to ensure the night isn't a total disaster. Daniel observes. Always. Taking time to consider every expression, all the body language and every single word, his mind works at an extraordinary speed in social matters. Daniel and Jeremy are quite unique. They consider everyone and when they encounter people, they have an ability to consider their lives, loves and above all, their concerns. They occasionally try to incorporate this into their work, to encourage all people to consider everyone. It is becoming more difficult, even unconventional, in journalism to sell the idea that we should have open minds and to at least consider opposing viewpoints and these two bright talents have moved into another realm in their work.

It's fair to say that the focus of tonight's gathering holds a lofted perch in the group. But how can a man of such mild intent wear those massive boots? A man who lives with such an unfathomably high level of self-awareness, kindness and consideration be totally inept in any type of personal appearance? 'These boots are a modern-day big hat!', Jeremy had said when warned about them in the office a few weeks ago. He says some crazy things at times, totally unexpected and occasionally quite vicious. But he is forgiven. The other side of that coin has a glorious shine. He has a troubled past, never knew his father and has no trace of information about him. Mark sees his eyes shine under the doorway entrance and wonders if that happens to everyone.

"You made it here ok then?" Mark shouts, alerting everyone present as if on purpose.
This brought a few smiles as Jeremy lives in a room upstairs.

"You might be wondering why I invited you all here this evening. Seriously though, you're the only people I... know!"

The pause and follow-up brought a bigger laugh than the opening line. Smiling, Jeremy then finished the sentence.

"Who turns up to work with their eyes open, let alone their minds?"

The smiles around the table contain waves of appreciation for the compliment. When Mark asks if Jeremy's cat will be joining them, he is met with a ripple of shush from the team, though he knows that the cat is kept secret from the landlord.

John makes his way from the bar with a tray of drinks.

"You'd all get the 'selected drinks' if I had my way," he shouts, while then appreciating the wails of laughter at his self-mocking northern tightness. He goes on.

"Order on-line!? What the hell is that about? I'm here, at the bar with my order and my money, what more do they want from me? Oh yeah, to go back to my table and use the app! What the?"

These were characters to amuse any establishment, not just their own group.

"I'm off for a piss. Or maybe they want me to do that on-line as well!?"

9.20pm Friday September 19th.

The football and the usual banter dispensed with earlier than usual, the tribe enter the second half of the night. The periphery let loose to the far end of the bar or out onto the street allows the conversation to evolve.

"Jeremy's leaving do! Who'd 'ave thought? Well, everyone!" quipped Mark, referring to the volatile nature of his close friend as well as the numerous official warnings for his supposedly poor professionalism.

"You think you're funny. Who should I be? If I am not myself in life then I am already dead." Jeremy's response didn't cause more than a ripple. The group know him well.

He is, tonight, very much alive but in their minds, he will soon be dead! Briefly. They have their own roads, the betting site adverts on the screen testify to that and provide another stimulus to cover this old ground. Jeremy didn't gamble and even once flicked the switch on all their lunchtime screens mid-bet. The second time, he launched a self-written virus to disrupt the sites they were using. They used their phones after that and were well aware of the gap that had appeared since they were university minded and drawing their roadmaps to the promised lands. There's a bitter taste for some and it's not just the relatively cheap beer. Their friend has been forced out, made an example of, somewhat. For their lack of support in the heated hours they feel a little guilt. But there is no animosity here and certainly no bridges that need to be built.

"A toast," says Luke, the only one left of the inner circle who hasn't made the gesture. "To Jezza, may he find fulfilment in the world of art. Oh and the protest groups too!"

The group laugh, somewhat awkwardly in parts, knowing Luke's disapproval.

"We seem to have an absence of beer" shouts Mark, not wanting the awkwardness to prevail.

"Yeah, and pizza," was the predictable reinforcement from Johnathan that surely would send the night along an even and faultless track. Their wishes came crashing from the tracks as Jeremy stood to speak. This group was expecting a speech and not one of them expected it to be something they could describe as 'normal'. None of them expected it to be uncontroversial and this feeling was cemented by the thoughtful and serious expression displayed by their unelected leader. Jeremy leaned forward slightly. A single sheet of paper drawn from his pocket, Jeremy opened it and the group saw short lines of less than a page. This was a relief to many and

Luke in particular. The paper was then placed on the table and not referred to or even glanced towards.

"We are in the battlegrounds my friends.
In the factories in boiler suits
 -of armour.
In the offices in business suits
 -of armour.
We have our swords and shields.
Return home with our wounds.
-from the brown-site fields we daily leave behind.
Sit in our caves and hide.
With our scars of flesh and mind.
We fight so hard and for so long.
The purpose? We can no longer truly say.
The day, the light, the way, they curl up and sleep now, their existence away.
We exist in the absence of awareness.
Of truth.
We are in the absence of bread and wine my friends"

"Told ya," said John, "pizza, it is," and made for the bar in a silent sigh and draughty relief.
Jeremy calls over to him,

"John! visit the south face of your mind, see what's growing there, who knows what you might find?" then walks across the wet floor, already mopped. Dan picks up his pen and writes the words down. Not the ones on the sheet, that is already in his possession! Jeremy's off-the-cuff follow-up to John was pure gold for Dan, who confirms to himself with a quick scan that the delivered speech matched the words on the sheet perfectly.

Matt's round birthed a beer-mat opportunity. Matt used to write poems with Jeremy on anything they could find and location often left just the beer-mats. Jeremy confides in Matt.

"After the incident with the computers. I knew I was alone. It's fine. I'd have preferred to keep fighting from that position but being alone and getting fired has its advantages. There are many people I know. Connections. I have to be patient but I am now in a position to engineer large-scale change.

"You actually want a revolution? Don't you? How do you like them? Extremely slow and simmering, maybe every 300 or so years?"

It's fair to say Matt's response was a shock to Jeremy but it didn't worry him in terms of confidentiality although it was clear that he was to receive no support.

"That's not even evolution!! Jeremy responded, a little too loud and with an appealing and outstretched palm.

"We are adding bits of plaster and paint to a mansion of such beauty. A mansion that is sinking into the ground and crumbling like a sand castle in a late summer storm. Looks fine from a distance though, from a party conference, when the votes are due in. Maybe evolution will be enough for you but it isn't what history tells us!" A moment of eye contact generates enough concern for Jeremy to leave the conversation with his subdued response.

"In answer to your question: no, I don't".

Luke, not even attempting to pretend he hadn't heard, returns to the gambling incident.

"I dunno, man. If I were you, I'd want answers," said Luke, taking up the challenge but has to follow Jeremy to the bar to pursue the logic he requires. Jeremy is philosophical.

"Had it coming. It's to be expected. Besides, I'll have time to concentrate on other things, ya know? I can always get back into it, but not in mainstream, they won't touch me now."

Luke won't accept this. He wants his friend back and part of the reason is a fear he feels for him.

"We all know your views. It doesn't make sense. Your views are in print every week. How the hell can they do this? How can you be compromising your neutrality by being involved in protests? You don't have any neutrality to compromise!"

Jeremy finds not only a comforting loyalty in Luke's words but a great deal of humour too. With a genuine laugh, Jeremy replies.

"Honestly, it's fine. Listen," he says, leaning into his close friend, "I've accessed the media feed. I will wait for the right time and I will blow the place apart. They'll be running around that place like sinners at the gates of hell. Other places too!"

Luke's open gaze was enough for Jeremy to seek his confidentiality, which he received unreservedly.

11.05pm Friday September 19th.

Jeremy returns to the table where only 3 remain, glances at Dan's writing pad with a smile. Dan writes and writes, but most is commentary. Takes his work home but in reality, it's just his addiction to writing. Writes about everything he's doing and even has his tablet with him at the table tonight. Dan's role in the business is more mundane yet he is a future editor as a result, perfect as the monitoring eye, like a drone in the sky, has no explicit opinions, untouchable, unknowable. Quite the opposite of Jeremy.

Jeremy has had enough to drink but has been pleased with his restraint in terms of information. He glanced at the screen for the first time since the match finished.

"They fight the social war and disappear to the extremes of the Earth. We've had a thousand years of opportunity. The time is up. There are battles in the four corners of the earth... North, south, east, west and what happens then? Wars and rumour of wars and then... 'we will protect you'! They all destroy each other on the other side of the world! Last night's news was a comic strip broadcast more appropriate for kids' hour. Oh! let's not bother the people with potential extinction events, just show them a celebrity accusation or a privileged aristocrat watching someone dance. Is it the broadcaster? Or the people? Or the people with power? Or all of them? Enlightenment, where the hell are you now!? Poets and painters? Musicians yeah, good, but lyricists? My God!"

The small group now listen intently. Jeremy has a way of finding great phrases when he goes on a rant, the sort of phrases they can only occasionally find while writing.

"Remember 4 years ago? Slow news years. Now, after a story lasting 2 years that is one of the extinction candidates, another two candidates dominate the news. We had the virus and there will be others. Now we have the climate and the prospect of a world war based on political ideology! Our main problem is people make money out of each crisis."

Sometimes it appears that Dan is disconnected but he still hears every word. He looks through the window at Jeremy's cat, strolling along the gantry behind the pub. The open window of his room is enough to provide him with a world of opportunity. Dan thinks of his friend in the same way. The window has been opened. Jeremy went on.

"At least, they do when they're allowed to! People watch the performance or they are fed from their phones and they don't truly listen or read, they don't absorb it, relate to it, link it to all the other knowledge they have. They see a story and... it's just there, a stand-alone abstract phenomenon right beside them in the fog. The news stories to them are like the mythical beasts invented to dissuade any village venturers hundreds of years ago. If we all stay where we are and do our jobs everything will be fine." Another rant that Dan absorbs into his tablet.

These three friends feel privileged to witness this final stage of the evening. Matthew remembers all the words his friend has written, whether it's in the weekly paper or the leaflets or the books. The books have a modest circulation and an admiring following. He told him his recent rhyme of 'statue of liberty' with 'anonymity' was brilliant. But Jeremy said it was a big regret and that he should have simply referred to the monument as the Statue of Anonymity and the rhyme would still exist.

"Don't be afraid to use what is already in people's heads," he said.

They all knew Jeremy was the artist. A truly great writer. Yet his advice was always meant well and heart felt, never arrogant.

Jeremy picks up Dan's tablet and begins to read out loud. This close group happy with this idea. The tablet is used for Dan's edited and more refined writing. Jeremy is particularly pleased with the content and begins to read in a more dramatic fashion as a result:

"The news plays out on the silenced screen but is largely ignored in this mundane scene. 10.00pm and just two hours left until tomorrow, well at least for us. Matt has nothing more to say after drinking the night away and Luke's been sinking 'em faster than usual for a Friday. The war latest, the forest fires, the election is skating on a sheet of ice, the demonstrations, deceit and the lies."

There are nods and smiles of approval, even from Matt who, after all, can't argue with facts. Jeremy skips to another part:

"The drones sink the ships, the winds fan the flames and water and bombs fall from the planes."

"My betrayal resulted in a meeting of long knives. Yes, someone told them lies. The clue is in the promotion shortly after. Plotting insurrection indeed!?"

Jeremy was ready for more disclosure and the group waited eagerly.

"I do know that one man wanted to do the deed among the desks. A show of strength and to show you the head on the stick as a deterrent. This was thought a risk, that there would be anger and revolt".

"They'd have lost half the staff!," said Matt, now fully attentive and looking as sober as he has for an hour.

"They'd have replaced them," Jeremy responded.

It was Luke's turn to take this up with surprising passion.

"But to revolt? Take to the streets, speak to the other publishers, a press revolution, saving our free speech and democracy!"

Jeremy, as resigned as they've ever seen him and yet also strangely resolute, responded.

"True, that would hurt them. It would worry them. But their true master is the government. A press revolt is fine but how many would be happy to be controlled and secure their future existence? Pushed too far, this would result in a controlled media and a free speech that becomes extinct. Months is all it would take. Save our democracy? We need to find one to save first."

Matt, adding with deep thought and a little mysticism, "You render to the state what is the state's. What do you render to what you believe in?"

Luke shouts to the bar for champagne and the others are laughing. He goes with Matt to collected the glasses and bottle. They both find the conversation invigorating.

"That pub in Keswick, what's it called?" says Luke. There's a pause in which both knew it was simply a time for Luke to think.

"The Justice of the Common Pleas," said Luke loudly, alerting the other two at the table.

"It's just as it was! A courtroom with the dock and everything. You can sit with a meal and drink in that room, just round by the cells, or even in a cell," he said excitedly. The others chuckled as the point had been made with the mere description of the place. Matt, with an outstretched hand and gesture, indicated to Jeremy his confusion at Luke's decision to splash out on champagne at this particular point in conversation.

"It nice. I have to be gracious," said Jeremy.

As Luke and Matt returned, Jeremy began again.

"Some of these people Dan, they will spend their final years fishing for redemption. It will be a hungry search. I pity them. I fear the blank page, we all do. But the greatest writing is still blank if it isn't read. I also fear the blank screen. The greatest broadcasts, ignored, are as useful as blank screens. The programs broadcasted at peak times, to me are blank screens."

The three now listened as if every word was historic. There was inspiration hanging all around the table.

"One day I believe that people will gather in this great establishment and will stay through the night, watching the news, discussing, even with strangers. This will be their home and cathedral, as it is mine. The people will come with their fake innocence and genuine concern. Such will be the times they find themselves in. But for now, as always, the screen is blank again."

Luke and Matt take this profound statement as the time to leave. Maybe they thought it would be a shame to end on a lesser note. Maybe it was just about closing time being only 10 minutes away.

"To the future," shouted Luke, necking the last of his Champagne. The four of them stood at the table, feet sticking to the midnight carpet like a hot summer tarmac. Stuck in their present moment, oblivious to their fates. No Idea just how bad and good things are going to get.

Seed Sower (The Boy in the Shed)

December 1942

It's a morning filled with such intense fear that it will remain with Billy for his final 3 years. While walking on the quiet but longer route for the bus to school, hands in pockets and arms tucked in close against the cold, down through fields between wet and cold stone walls, Billy suddenly stands completely still and stares straight ahead. As the winter breeze stops breathing with him, Billy reaches out one hand and touches the cold damp stones of the wall beside him: feeling for some stability. Everything is threatening. The bare black branches arming themselves down to the black but recently golden leaves. The shadowing crows are the size of fighter planes. Billy feels like he is the only human left alive.

An hour later and Billy sits on the cold ground, back against the wall that supported him, his hand on the bag of books he'd dropped. He is so scared of life for these long minutes and is still recovering. He knows he won't be at school today and wants to be back in the garden shed at his aunt's house.

Billy returned to the house and was relieved that his aunt was there, in her usual position by the fire. He stood and looked into the flames for both warmth and calm.

"I really couldn't go to school today, Aunty. Sorry," Billy said to his smiling aunt, who hadn't even suggested any requirement for an explanation.

"Take off that bag and sit down," she said quietly. "Are you alright?"

"I just got really scared on the way. Is Dorothy alright?"

"Yes, she's upstairs asleep." Billy got up and went to check on Dorothy. The beautiful, white and grey cat woke from her sleep on the bed as Billy walked into his room. His growing attachment to Dorothy had outpaced his two months living with his aunt and the cat had gravitated toward Billy despite her ten years in the house. Billy arched himself around his friend for a while.

It was almost lunchtime when Billy went to spend some time in the garden shed. He was still scared and confused but this was his favourite place. He had big plans for the spring and had been busy repairing and painting the neglected shed.

A host of visions haunted Billy, blackened in the isolation of the fields at midnight. The stone wall, the mud, the whole horrifying event burst into the room, shattering the windows into his head. Billy laid awake for hours in his bed. He thought about his life so far. He could remember events from when he was just two years old, but he had learnt to not talk about it. The day's events also caused Billy to remember two other times that he was scared to something like the same degree. It was strange to him that the other two occasions both had specific reasons and yet this time, there wasn't one.

One time was being pinned down by bullies on the way home from school. This felt horrific at the time and he remembers the stinging tears and his raw eyes hurting in the cold. It was five years ago and Billy was only seven and was suffering at school, largely because he was very quiet and somewhat misunderstood by children and adults alike. If Billy didn't have anything to say he would not speak and at times, for long periods, he had nothing to say. Other times, Billy spoke in a forthright manner and spoke the truth as he saw it, even when most people wouldn't.

The other time was in a graveyard and Billy was remembering it once again. Every word. Billy was sat against the back of a headstone one beautiful afternoon, admiring the view and inventing phrases for a new story when he heard this hushed conversation not far behind him:

"I did a job in London. Got rid of some evidence here."

"Where?" came the other voice, a little deeper.

"When I tell you this, you'll know I should be on the next job. He's in there. Been there four years."

"So, where the hell is she?"

"Oh. She's still in there, just above him." There was a pause before the same voice continued.

"You see, when you're really not scared. When you're desperate. You just do it and take a massive risk. The consequences don't scare me. Then, cos I was lucky, it turned out safer than anything else. Someone else might burn it in some woods and they catch up with him. Not me, nobody's gonna find this guy, he'll be there another hundred years at least." There were quiet gasps and sniggers.

"That was a big risk, digging down another two feet in the night."

"It wasn't at night, it was straight after the burial." There was more hushed laughter.

"What!?"

The voice of the first man was vaguely familiar to Billy. This was a frightening moment in Billy's life but he wanted so much to see the man, or at least the woman's gravestone. He wanted the man to be caught. His hands gripped the blades of grass where he sat staring ahead at the trees that had looked so lovely a few minutes ago. His heart was exploding inside him and his stomach felt like it was dissolving. Billy leaned slowly to his left and prayed there were no twigs to snap as he put out his hand. Peering around the stone that had stood between him and the men, relieved that neither was facing him, he first made a mental note of the grave they stood by. Then, trying to identify the man, he understood that, had the men been facing him for a convenient identification, they would surely see him. Billy leaned back into position. It was the perfect time to look as there were no voices. Billy knew the men had started walking and had his greatest fear of the whole episode: that the men were walking in his direction. It took another minute of absolute terror for Billy to be sure they had walked off in the direction of the village.

Billy hadn't recalled this event in such detail since the year it happened. With this memory, surfacing as it did, along with the day's events, Billy knew that he was to get no sleep tonight. He knew that, with sleep he would dream about the events of the morning and it could reveal some reasons for the fears he had. He loved dreaming, even when the dreams were bad - but this wasn't something he wanted this time. There will also be no need to wake and be forced to relive the nightmare of its reality. To feel it all over again. This has happened many times and Billy began to think about how his dreams inspired him and how they sometimes even revealed the truth to him. But with no sleep, he was content with only one thing: there would be no nightmares tonight. Billy began to write a poem called 'The Fear'.

> *This winter stripped flesh from the trees.*
> *Monuments of wood, to the dead it leaves.*

Before The Fear and the start of Billy's final 3 years, in the early summer of 1942 there would be much to experience and influence in life. There would be very little school, decreasing as the war went on. At a time when children were attacked with a cane merely to remind them that they're followers or to beat out even a shadow of individuality, Billy's persona condemned him to suffer far more than most. The war caused even more alienation. Billy was living in a large house, full of children, some now at school, fathers at war, mothers working in the war effort, some with no parents at all. Billy had a unique understanding of humanity for a boy of 12. Devoting a great deal of attention to the details of life, Billy was considered to be quite different by teachers as well as peers and for this he sometimes paid a heavy price. Living in a large and beautiful house in the country was something he often reminded himself of, hoping that it would bring some calm appreciation. It didn't.

There were many children living in the house who were unfortunate to have no available or suitable guardians while their fathers were at war. The children who Billy knew well were the most unfortunate and especially the younger ones. He instinctively found those that had lost their parents and spent time helping them with daily matters. This attributed purpose and meaning to Billy but the lack of close family was the worst possible scenario for him. Shy and scared, Billy often withdrew deep into his own mind, exploring his thoughts and creating his unique understanding of the world. His knowledge was extraordinary, both in and out of school. However, he rarely demonstrated this in school as he spoke so little, struggling to answer questions in class due to the pressure of attention. Test results revealed only average abilities as Billy was not compatible with this situation either. Billy's intelligence wasn't fully understood by anyone but had a level of recognition from only two people. Alice and her brother, Jack, were his best and, realistically, only friends. They managed to create the environment that Billy required in order to feel comfortable and reveal something close to his true identity. School wasn't compulsory at Billy's age in these times but it's what his mother would have wanted. Father ensured that Billy was able to continue when he left for duty. By the summer and the latter stages of another school year, there was a reduced schedule of lessons which still occurred in the basement and many children no longer attended. For Billy, this was all to end before too long.

Billy had always synchronised his watch every morning with the large clock in the hall and waited for the school bus. He was greatly missing routines in his life and had started to fill the spaces with new ones. Alice and Jack were always beneath the clock waiting for the synchronisation to be complete.

One particular day that Billy would always remember well, began near the children hopscotching through the gates. It was because of a rare conversation with Jack about the war. However, this couldn't happen while another boy was present. Jack's friend, Joe had decided to commit to introducing himself to Billy. Joe was a good and honest lad but had an image to maintain. He managed this well with his remarkable communication skills but had a feeling of regret that all this was preventing him from becoming Billy's friend. He had witnessed events of bullying towards Billy and not helped or reported anything.

"Billy, it's short for William," was the statement from Joe that took Billy completely by surprise.

"But it's not, is it?" replied Billy, who hadn't any desire to befriend Joe. "It's a completely different word. Joe is short for Joseph, I mean, 'Will' is fine but it's nothing like 'Billy,' it's not something you can spew out with the standing start of a closed mouth!". Joe, open mouthed, was both stunned and intrigued by Billy's reaction.

"Well, erm Will, I'll keep that in mind," said Joe as he turned to join some friends, one of them shouting out to him before he got close enough that a normal speaking voice would be adequate.

"What you talking to Sludge for?" he called with a loud laugh. Sludge was one of the names given to Billy because he always had dirt on his trousers from sitting down on the grass and soil, often at the pond. Billy didn't mind too much but preferred 'Bush', the other name he'd been assigned due to his wavey and uncombed hair.

"I'm confused by the whole thing," said Jack, aware that the encounter with Joe was best kept brief for now at least. "Our fathers have to leave us and go to war for a while just so we can be like we were before. Were things so bad for everyone over there that they had to cause this?" Billy was trying to remember what had been discussed in class. He knew that through his consumption of books, magazines and news that he was more aware of these things than the other children and didn't want to upset his friend with any insights.

"Our lives must change for the worst before they return, as must theirs. Things have always been this way from time to time. I don't see that changing any time soon." Billy didn't speak like a boy of his age. His words were considered before spoken and sometimes even revealed themselves as if previously prepared on a page.

"I'm thinking of asking the teachers," continued Jack, "they don't talk about it enough for my liking. I want to know how it all happened. I want to know how it will end. They speak about it but I'm not sure if any of it is even true!". Billy nodded in agreement.

"Give it a try, but only in private, not in the lesson. I'll bet you anything you like that you will hear a repeat of what you've heard before. Why would they burden us with truth? They certainly wouldn't do that in any other country, so why here? We can't blame them, they want us to remain happy for as long as possible. If we get back to how we were then they were right to. We won't all get back to that though. In fact, thinking about it, none of us will." Jack looked shocked at Billy's words and Billy in turn looked shocked at Jack's reaction. Billy walked away with an initial feeling of guilt that was later to subside as he became convinced that he'd found the right level of compromise.

Reality is there, so clear in the blackest night.
But most days are misty and at school it disappears from sight.

Jack found Billy on the bus after school and told him he was right.

"Glad I didn't take the bet," he laughed. Billy's smile was all Jack needed as he knew there would be no words from his friend in the reduced privacy of the bus. The speech-free journey allowed a memory to resurface in Billy's mind from when the English teacher called him to the office about his story:

'Billy, the whole thing turned out to be a movie! The main character got up and walked out of the theatre. How did you come by this idea?'

'From Hamlet, Sir' was Billy's reply, despite them not reading it in school.

'It's nothing like it,' protested the teacher in a rather dismissive way.

'Yes it is, it's a play within a play. He did it to make the play feel like reality. Sometimes even life doesn't feel like reality.'

The teacher was full of admiration but showed only contempt, partly due to Billy's abrupt explanation. Billy had made a mental note under the event to remind him.

Jack and Billy got off the bus at the same place for once as Billy was happy to walk the extra distance to remain with his friend. Jack asked him how he deals with the abuse from other children and the teachers. They talked about the blackened eye he'd had and how it brought both ridicule and a certain respectability. Billy didn't mention the children but did explain how he copes with the teacher: "I tell myself he doesn't exist, I mean, he only partly exists anyway. He's just a machine, made to play a part, it's not his fault. It's the manufacturer's fault." Jack smiled, amused and amazed at the way his friend sees life.

In the final week of the school year and walking down the path to the bus with his friends, the conversation was upbeat among most children and with Jack, it revolved around the planned activities when the summer term was to end. There was a thought in Billy's head that kept him going. He wasn't sure if it was his own pure invention, something that his mind had created for his personal preservation. Billy believed that he would be rescued from the situation he found himself in. He wasn't sure how this would happen and didn't fully understand why he had ended up where he was. A lot of thought had been expended in this area. He'd been in trouble at school for writing poems in the back of his book and today he wrote about how the grass isn't greener on the other side but it was much easier to make that grass seem greener than to transform the brown grass where we are. The teacher had torn the page from the book and thrown it in the bin. Billy became visibly upset but most children simply laughed at him: it's what the teacher would have wanted.

At the end of the day, waiting for Jack, Billy saw Joe walking toward him and felt more nervous than usual due to the bad day he'd experienced. Joe began to smile as he got nearer and by the time he'd reached Billy, he had pulled out the crumpled page from his bag.

"I got this back for you," said Joe with a smiling face of achievement, "it's amazing!" Billy was filled with joy, not because he needed the paper or its contents. He could remember every word, after all. Billy knew he'd found someone else who appreciated his talents but who had also taken the risk to retrieve the words for him. Billy took the paper.

"Thank you! Thank you so much," he said.

"My pleasure, William," came the reply. Both boys laughed together.

"Joseph! Come with me and Jack, we will go down to the water for a while, we love the water." The three of them caught the bus and then enjoyed an hour at the water before heading back to the house.

That evening, Billy thought about Joseph's father who wasn't fighting in the war but was reporting. He wanted to read those reports. Getting that poem back was a source of joy and Billy remembered feeling this way when he wrote a poem on the blackboard before school started and all the class had read it before the teacher noticed. They'd thought it was part of a lesson. Billy's attention also switched to the small group of younger children who had begun to rely on him, sitting with them at meal time and talking with them until it was time to go to the rooms. Billy always took time to find Jack and Alice before bed. His circle of true friends, ones who he could be open with, was a circle of two. To Billy, it was a triangle and would never resemble a circle.

From October 1942 Billy had found himself in a far better place, both mentally and geographically. Living with an aunt and attending a version of school much smaller than before, it was as close to perfect as he could hope. Billy and his Aunt Bess became close and Billy enjoyed working through the large number of books in a spare room at his aunt's cottage as well as listening to the radio with her. Billy was attending school less often, spending much of his time there ensuring that the younger ones were coping. His closest companion, after his aunt, was now Dorothy, her beloved cat.

Missing only Jack and Alice from his previous life, Billy compensated with frequent letters, a form of communication that he was very comfortable with. Both Jack and Alice replied, ensuring the relationships continued. Over time, the friends grew even closer than when they were all together, such was the open nature of the letters and the depth of thought in Billy's writing. Something new arose from the communication, in the form of drawings. Alice, a very accomplished artist, was both amazed and delighted to discover Billy's talents. She was also confused that Billy had not previously revealed this talent, showing everyone a particular drawing of a large truck that Billy called the 'Juggerthought', although while he was thinking about the war it was named the 'think tank'. Finally, the idea was to be a 'well-articulated lorry' that should visit schools and inform children on thinking and philosophy. Alice and Jack loved the little children's story that was attached to it. The irony was not lost on them when they discovered their teacher liked it too as these vehicles were still a new phenomenon. Jack had seen Billy's drawings before and while he had told Alice about them, she never saw them. Alice had an appreciation not only of Billy's talent for drawing but of the depth of thought in his work and remembered the time he said that he had so much work to do.

Billy shared his communication with his friends willingly and openly with his aunt and they talked at length about many things. Bess soon realised that Billy had many questions but also many answers. She had explained that the land was a working farm when she was a child and this explained the machinery in the field and the skeleton of a barn even further away. Billy asked about his uncle and Bess told him that he was serving in the same place as Billy's father.

"I'd like to know more about the war," said Billy, knowing that there wouldn't be much his aunt could add.

"Yes William, we will listen to the news more often. I think you should do some writing about what you discover."

"Yes, we should do that. I'd love to know more, in time for their return."

"We will learn together."

As Billy listened to the radio and worked through the books, he started to write increasingly large amounts and Bess was intrigued by the chaotic content of it all but this began to change over the following weeks. Billy began to formulate his thoughts into topics and had his own large box full of files. He began to tidy and dig the garden using the old tools in the shed. New tools arrived and the work continued through the winter.

The cold days didn't stifle Billy's progress with the garden and his reading and writing began to take up every evening. He loved the winter as much as any other season and was able to see the beauty in it. The rain was wonderful except for the smell of wet coats in the school cloakroom. The snow was beautiful but reminded him of snowballs hitting him in the face in the school yard. He loved the frost and its complexity but also that it captured moisture and turned it into something beautiful. Billy would see all the sunrises his sleep would allow and in winter would see far more of them. He loved them all except the midwinter ones that climbed over the school yard wall and stretched pink window frames across the classroom. He wrote a poem about the young children's voices being unheard as if their winter scarves were permanently over their mouths. He loved the water and remembered a pond from his earlier life and one afternoon he'd sat there and wrote 'the rain started so hard it bubbled the pond like a laboratory of creation'. His father etched the words onto some wood and mounted it on the wall. He wanted the water to freeze so he could slide on it but December was to be mostly mild and a time of great reflection with many walks to the water for contemplation.

A winter child, warm and duffled.
Social-scarfed voices, born muffled.

By January 1943 and now almost 13, Billy had grown much closer to his Aunt Bess, who had developed a natural understanding of her nephew. She had explained that she'd been trying to locate him since his father had left. At least, that's what she said. Billy's recollection didn't correlate well with this. He remembered her from when he was about 4 years old, talking to his father in the kitchen. Her husband was there and she was saying 'Oh, sorry, I don't comment on everything. If I have nothing to say, I say nothing' and Billy liked this. Bess was the sister of Billy's mother. He never knew his mother. His memories of his aunt were cloudy and he wasn't sure why there was so little to remember as this was unusual for him. Billy was aware that his aunt spoke about his mother with a great deal of love in her voice but this made him even more aware that she spoke so little of his father.

"Your father is a wonderful man, William. Warm and caring. We must hope that he is sent home soon." One of the first difficult questions that Bess was to become accustomed to, arrived at this moment.

"If a soldier dies in the war, how long is it before his family is told?" Bess was yet to fully appreciate Billy's forthright nature and the depth of his understanding. Billy knew the answer and had anticipated the answer that his aunt might provide.

"Well, that depends," said Bess. "It depends on, well, where and how it happens."

Billy waited until the evening to show his aunt some writing he'd done. He told her it was for school and Bess happily read through his work, smiling often with a show of admiration. Further confirmation of her general approval was made verbally before Billy went to bed, leaving Bess to pick out more of Billy's poems. She started to read one about the garden flowers in the spring. One of the pieces was much darker than the others as well as presenting a more adventurous and advanced style. It sparked a certain concern within Bess. She read it again.

> *The Fear.*
> *My mother is dead, taken the same day as my sister.*
> > *At least that's what they said. I don't*
> *remember and yet I miss her.*
> *This winter stripped flesh from the trees.*
> *Dead monuments of wood it leaves.*
> *Like I was frozen in a photograph.*
> *Stuck in a time I cannot move forwards from.*
> > *Mud sucking my shoes downwards, the*
> *clouds stopped.*
> *Choking in a winter scarf, the sun stopped.*
> > *Sinking under the life of the morning*
> *sunbathed surface path.*
> *Into a long dark night.*
> *Grasping the cold, wet stone.*
> *The sharpness and threatening timelessness of it.*
> > *The immensity of its existence touched my*
> *fleeting flesh.*
> > *Dark and demonic ancient burial earth,*
> *dead and decaying.*
> *Between the world's walls, this dirty bed.*
> *Stoney, six feet fallen bony bed.*
> *At least that's what they said.*

The next day, as Billy was shoveling coal out of the bunker, Bess called him in and sat him down on the sofa close to Dorothy to give him some news. She was shaking and Billy sensed the emotions and was already preparing himself for something that would amount to confirmation of what he already knew. Bess explained that she had wanted to tell him since he moved in but didn't know how.

"Your heroic father died in a large battle. I received the news only two weeks ago." Billy's eyes filled with tears but he remained in control. Had he received the news before moving to be with his aunt, this couldn't have been achieved.

"When?" said Billy, looking at the fireplace.

"I don't know," said Bess, "in the last two months. We heard from him in November and I got the letter in early

January. The letter doesn't say. I have been trying to tell you but we... well, we've only just started out here." Bess handed Billy the letter. He read the four lines. The words were branded in his mind.

"I know," said Billy. "It was December 2nd and I have been grieving ever since."

"Oh William," said Bess, putting her arm around his shoulders. "You can stay here as long as you want. I don't want to be here on my own but if you eventually leave, that's fine, I'll just have to get some help."

Billy had been here only a few months and Bess decided it was right not to ask about Billy's comment that he knew all along. Billy didn't ask why his uncle wouldn't be home to help his aunt after the war. The two of them talked about Billy's childhood for a while and then moved on to Billy's plans for the garden shed. They took the long walk to the bottom of the garden, something that took Bess some time and effort due to complex medical conditions. Plans for the planting of seeds in the spring were discussed as well as to make the interior a nice place for Billy to spend time writing and drawing.

Billy obeyed most of his aunt's instructions but he actually saw them as advice and was to oppose two main pieces of advice to wild extremes. They were to not go beyond the garden walls and to not talk to strangers. Billy loved the garden and right from arriving he had planted many seeds that he'd found in the shed. Bess was unable to tend the garden anymore and the seeds were a few years old.

In early May, the garden was already filling with flowers to the delight of Billy and his aunt. The shed had been repaired and painted by Billy thanks to his time at school being further shortened and he also managed to decorate the interior with drawings and poems. Some of the many books in the house were moved to the new shelves in the shed and Billy was reading more than ever. A whole shelf was devoted to history books. The top shelf contained his favourite books: 'Alice's Adventures in Wonderland' and 'The Wonderful

Wizard of Oz' were both about dreams. Billy loved the gap: the space between sleep and awake, finding it rewarding in its insightfulness and as a source of creativity. Apart from these books, Billy's favourite was a book about flowers. It was called 'Garden Flowers' and Billy loved it even more because the bright blue cover was so worn and he found this inspiring as he knew his aunt had used it many times and possibly took it out into the garden too. He knew his aunt's favourite flowers and, following a secret visit to the local village, Billy planted more seeds, some that he acquired as well as some plants that he managed to wheel back on the long route from the village in the barrow that he'd repaired. Bess knew he'd been to the village and was reluctant to be too harsh with him as the visit was to buy her items for the garden. She was confused how much he'd got from the small amount of money he had and trusted that he wouldn't be going back.

      One beautiful and warm Sunday morning, Billy woke very early and opened the window to the crowing dawn with a degree of excitement. He greeted Dorothy in the kitchen and gave her a little food from yesterday's dinner. She didn't eat it and Billy knew that her night of hunting had been successful. After a walk round the garden, Billy made some tea for his aunt who had begun to stir upstairs.

      "I'm off to the water today," Billy said leaving little room for protest.

      "That's fine," came the reply from the top of the stairs. "Do you mean all day?".

      "It could be, I'll take some sandwiches."

It wasn't long before Billy set off with his chocolate rations and was sat by the water well before mid-day. This was a place where a few people would be seen, especially on a Sunday morning. Especially this Sunday morning. The air was filled with the beautiful country smells of a warm day in May. The warm soil, the farm and the fresh-cut grass from a mile down the lane in the village. The first person that Billy saw was an old man called Henry. He was a lonely man and yet knew many people. Henry said 'good morning' to Billy as he walked by with his dog.

"Good morning, Sir," said Billy. "Good morning, Mollie," he said to the dog.

"You know my dog?" said Henry with a smile.

"I've seen you calling her. Are you from the village?" Billy quickly enquired.

"Yes. I've seen you there too."

"I'd love to come to the fair, could I come and help"? said Billy with an expression pleading approval.

"I'm sure you could! I'm also sure you would without my consent too."

Billy smiled and stood up from his corner plot of grass. He knew, just as well as Henry, that to walk into the village together would be a great way to be accepted as a member of the village and to find some worthwhile jobs to do. The two of them walked towards the village and they both chuckled as they walked by the sign advertising the fair. Billy was soon working in the main stalls with three other children, all younger than him. Florence, Annie and Tom lived in the small house on the edge of the village, a little isolated from the main road. Florence was over-heard by Billy talking with Henry who had said Billy was from the cottage in the fields up the lane. Florence had said that she'd love to live out there but mother was already scared to be on the edge of the village.

Billy later told the children he was actually from the town. Billy recognised Tom from the schoolhouse as he had helped him with his shoes but attendance was so sporadic from many children that some relationships for Billy never really developed. Annie and Florence had not attended. Billy visited the village the next morning and helped to tidy up from the fair. He gave flowers to the two girls that he'd picked on the way over. He said his own flowers would be ready in a few weeks and he'd bring some for their mother.

When Margaret, the children's mother, received her flowers she watched Billy wander into the village and didn't see him come back for three more hours. She then watched him walk over towards the town. As his head disappeared from sight, it reappeared again behind another wall and he was clearly walking in another direction. Margaret realised that her daughter was right and decided to visit the cottage.

A week later, Margaret visited the cottage. She walked through the beautiful garden and saw Billy building a new fence.

"Hello," said Billy in a slightly questioning manner and in one word had managed to express his surprise along with a certain hope that Margaret didn't blow Billy's cover too much.

"Good afternoon, Billy. Nice work. I've come to say thanks for your help!"

The door opened on her arrival and Margaret produced flowers for Bess. The two of them went inside. They talked and drank tea together for an hour once Bess had put the flowers in a vase.

"I don't think you realise what Billy brings to the village," said Margaret. "You will of course, know just how remarkable he is."

"He certainly is," agreed Bess, yet wanting more information.

"Florence described to me this week how she's getting more like Sandy every day. Now, Sandy is a fox, in a story. It would appear that Billy told the whole story to the children at the fair."

"Goodness," said Bess, "It's not one I'm aware of."

"That doesn't surprise me. You see, it was as if... it was as if, the whole story was created right at that time, just for my children. Sandy was a fox cub living with her mother and two siblings and had decided that she was old enough to start making a big effort around the den and help her mother." Bess was full of anticipation. "There's more. Sandy's brother, I forget the name, was a really good scratcher and marked all the trees around the den for protection. I've recently reprimanded Tom for engraving 'Tommy West lives here' on the fence. The day after the fair, he sanded it off and repainted it. He told me he was only trying to mark our area and protect us and that he's going to draw pictures for me instead and asked if I would put one on the fence."

Bess held back a small tear. She knew that Billy was capable of creating a story like this but not so quickly after meeting the children and talking with them.

> *My flowers are the memories of the seed I sowed.*
> *I love the sowing even more than the flower.*

By late July, the garden was full of flowers, vegetables and fruit, as too were the house and shed! Billy had clearly returned to the village a few times. Bess heard stories from him about a man he had met there called Jim but this didn't concern her too much as Jim had previously visited the house in his capacity as a plumber. Bess did know people from the village but hadn't been there for a few years and all her supplies were now brought by van from the town.

Bess listened to Billy's stories in the evenings and began to recall people from the village. This was merely coincidental to her until he mentioned Jane. Bess recognised elements of Jane's past and began to think that Billy had changed the names of real people and that some of the stories he'd written were in fact true.

"You know quite a few people from the village, William." Bess stated without a hint of questioning. Billy didn't feel any awkwardness and promptly replied.

"Yes, quite a few." He thought it was the end of the matter but Bess returned to the issue after a few more references to stories and poems, prompting Billy to continue.

"Everyone there knows me, Aunty! I love going there." Billy was hopeful that this full confession of his activity and desires would allow him to continue his visits without causing distress, although he had no intention of stopping his excursions. Bess took a look around the room at Billy's drawings and poems.

"It's fine, I understand. It's obviously been happening so long that you've proved you're safe going there. It's a 40 minute walk and is good exercise too." Bess was fully aware of the impact that the experiences had on Billy and that it had become a source of inspiration. She was not yet aware however, of the source of inspiration that Billy had become for the village.

Bess had recently had a meeting with Billy's teacher about remarks in class and a piece he had written, so she was reluctant to enquire about where Billy got many of his ideas from. The subsequent talk that Bess had with Billy revealed a very deep and sensitive nature within him. In the days and weeks that followed the meeting, Billy clearly reflected on his actions and wanted to learn more about himself as well as the expectations of those around him. He knew that he needed to speak the truth a little less in order to avoid upsetting people but the alternative needed to be silence and not another version of what he wanted to say. Reflecting and analysing was a regular activity and Billy had become an expert but the adaptations he intended to make in his own character rarely materialised.

It was shortly after the story of Jane that Bess joined Billy one evening sat outside the shed for, what was to become a few delightful hours. She had found him looking particularly thoughtful that afternoon, scowling at the plants.

"Could I read it?" Bess asked in a particularly gentle way. Billy handed his aunt the words he was writing.

"It's just some ideas. I'll complete it tonight. I always complete things at night, it's much easier."

> *Each year, out of here, walk the unborn.*
> *Saplings Marching by, unknown.*
> *The once friendly flower headed winter weeds.*
> *Are turncoats full of poisonous seeds.*

Bess knew Billy well enough to suspect that this could be about his experiences in school and possibly his opinions of school as a system. It was a damning account and yet beautifully written. Bess was extremely impressed with the maturity of the writing but was more focused on Billy's mood: he was clearly at a very low point. There were very few children still attending school, especially at Billy's age, and Bess decided that he should stay home.

"You are allowed to leave school William, because of the war. It's only a year early anyway and you can help with some house improvements. I don't think you should go back. You've learnt so much so quickly and you always will."

The evening was filled with laughter as well as deep conversation. They laughed about the farmer coming round and explaining to Bess that Billy had moved a mattress from his tip. Billy had dragged it to the side of the wall he jumped over to cushion his fall.

"He built the wall higher. It was too high to jump from," remembered Billy.

"Did he do that to stop you?"

"Not really. He did it to stop the sheep climbing onto the wall."

"How could they get up there?"

"They walked up the soil heap I created so I could get up easier!"

"Well, he didn't tell me that part!" said Bess, shaking her head with loud laughter.

Toward the end of the evening Bess told Billy that she was inspired by him and that she was to begin a major project of restoration on the house. Billy hadn't realised that his aunt was so wealthy and was excited about the plans.

"It will include an extension with en-suite bedroom and you can live there if you want to. You could find local work if you prefer, I'm sure you could, with your contacts." Billy smiled in amusement.

"I'll certainly stay for a while, thank you."

Billy had ten notes on the wall in the shed, among many other things. Bess had seen every item on the walls but this surprised her. The church wasn't a major feature in their lives so the notes caused some deeper contemplation. Bess sat with Billy very rarely in the shed, it was his space, but one time she looked at the notes while talking to Billy.

"We live in complicated times," said Bess in an attempt to address the notes. Billy's response, while looking at his aunt and then the notes was thoughtful.

"Things will get much more complicated. They always do."

"I have no idea where you get your wonderful stories," she said, "I adore the one about Jane and the delightful story of John, the local Santa. Such detail."

Billy began to speak and Bess noticed the word 'is' in his opening sentence and wondered if it was simply referring to the story he'd written.

"Jane is special, Auntie. It's not just because we share the same birthday, or that she loves to watch the river and the ducks. For my friends, if that's what they are, this would be a cup so special that it overflows with reasons. Jane is special for many reasons and one is that she's the widow of a pilot." Bess nodded in agreement. "I mean, that doesn't make her special. No!" said Billy in an unusually slightly raised voice. "She is special because she deals with it. She said: "They tell me I'll be fine" and "You must feel so proud" and..." Billy was getting a little excited and needed time to consider his words. Bess asked him what made Jane special and it was enough to push down Billy's relentless guard.

"Well, she said: "Damn them, time is a great healer if you will just give me the time. Call me Jane. Stop referring to me as Tom's widow". Jane is a hero. She does so much in the community and with a small child too. Coping with her husband's death wouldn't be so damned impossible if they treat her right." Bess brought calm back to the conversation by speaking softly.

"William, don't say that word." Billy replied, even more softly.

"Sorry, Aunty, I know. Nothing is 'impossible'." They both smiled.

In the daytime my thoughts are like the water vapour.
It condenses into water on the windows at night.
I wipe it off.

Continuing to ponder the big questions in life, Billy was seeking answers in new books and amongst the people that he knew. New books appeared all the time in the house. Bess wasn't pleased to find the words 'God is a tyrant' engraved on the inside of the shed door. She'd tell him it was offensive to her but that it was fine for him to write anything he wanted in his book. Billy sanded the words away and re-painted the shed door. He was aware of an emerging atheist within him but tried to resist. He never stopped waiting for a god, any god, to speak to him.

Bess was sat in her beautiful garden that Billy had created in his time at the house. She was sat in a wheelchair and was well into her tenth year living alone, although only five years without Dorothy, who had managed to reach her nineteenth year. The garden was very well maintained and contained all the varieties of flowers, fruit and vegetables that Billy loved to grow. Behind her was the beautiful cottage. The open sash window, air-filled cottage of sun-bathed walls is what Bess loved most of all.

A car came up the lane and parked beside the gate. Bess looked up with a calm and contented manner despite the extremely rare event. A man stepped from the car and walked to the gate. His black mirrored shoes clicking up the flower-hugged cobbles like clogs. Bess was curious but not alarmed. The man wore small, round spectacles and smart clothes, although his shirt sleeves were rolled up due to the hot weather.

"Mrs Thomson?" he called from the gate.
"You are?" Bess immediately enquired. The man apologised for not introducing himself first: "Oh

sorry madam. I'm George Brown and I'm a journalist".

Bess wheeled her chair and it rocked towards the gate. She briefly checked the paperwork being offered by means of identification. There was a long period of quiet, containing only bird song. It was almost a minute and George had transformed from the confident and educated writer that stepped from the car into a rather nervous young man.

"So, erm, could I step into the garden?" There was another pause before Bess replied:

"You can tell me why you're here." George remained at the other side of the gate and briefly explained the reason for his visit:

"I'm telling the story of Billy. A couple of people back in London met up recently and this story began to emerge. It's my first time around here, I mean, I know a few things already, not much. Then I, well, I drive up here and over Billy's Bridge." Said George with a smile. Bess waited for more information which needed her prompt:

"Who were they?"

"Just a couple of people from the village down the road, people he worked with. One was called Roger, I forget the other name," George added, "and then they contacted some others from the village and the town. I told my editor and he was interested enough to let me come down to do some research for a story for the paper. I hope you don't mind me surprising you with this." George anticipated the now predictable pause.

"Do you mind?" He said. Bess explained herself:

"I'm sorry, young man, I only speak when I have something to say. You hoped that I didn't mind and that's good. You ask if I mind and the answer is 'no'."

"Ah good, then." George continued, before he was interrupted:

"However, I need a few days," said Bess. George, nodding and repeating the word 'yes' was happy to retreat to his car at that moment and called out:

"A few days, yes, of course."

The second meeting, just two days later, took place in the garden. George arrived and stood at the gate again even though Bess was in the kitchen. He called out to her and she emerged to the garden in her chair. She laughed:

"Most people would come to the door."

"Well, the thing is, you were in the garden last time and.." George ran out of words to explain why he remained at the gate. Bess understood that he had politely left her that space last time and that this time, although it wasn't necessary, he couldn't bring himself to breech the gate.

Sat outside the impressive garden shed, they talked about the colourful garden that surrounded them and Bess explained that she has a gardener now, as well as help from local people. They went on to talk about Billy's work in the village. He'd worked with a carpenter from the middle of 1944 to the end of 1945 but did extra work in the local gardens and the park. The Education Act had raised the school leaving age to 15 a little after this. Billy was 14 and had just started a large job and was doing really well. He'd spent the previous year helping with the renovations and improvements on the house.

Now in the cottage, George made it clear that he knew of the death of Billy's father and that it had occurred on the same field and in the same week as her husband's death. He also explained much of what he'd heard about Billy: the friendships he'd made in the village; the stories and poems; the drawings. This was nothing new to Bess. She had many visitors from the village and Billy was mentioned all the time. She did wonder what she was expected to add to this story, apart from maybe the items she had kept and the obvious question that she had been expecting since they met.

"Everything is down here or in the shed. I had it all brought downstairs. I knew I would end up living in the extension one day," said Bess as she gave George the keys to the shed. He brought out a box for her, from the chest in the corner. They went through a few things: stories and drawings. These were physical confirmation of the verbal communications he'd had over the last two weeks with various people.

"A few people have visited me in the last 10 years," Bess confessed.

"I thought you'd had regular visitors and people helping."

"Oh, no. I mean people from outside the area. Strangers, interested in the story. That you're telling his story doesn't surprise me. There's a man from the village refers to William as a legend! But I'm surprised you've not asked what happened to William." George was stunned by the abrupt way Bess addressed the matter. The customary pause went by.

"You don't know?" asked George, tentatively. To anyone else it would have sounded like he knew. The reply was immediate:

"No! And neither do you, do you?" George admitted that he didn't but had a heavy sense of brinkmanship, smiling as he confronted his confusion and the question: 'How can she be so sure that I don't know?' he thought.

An hour was filled with stories of the shed, the garden and Billy's friends at school. Bess was a little more open now that she was aware of George's knowledge of these matters. She mentioned a few school friends and George expressed surprised and that he'd only heard about Jack and Alice. He was visibly alerted when Bess mentioned the depth of Billy's knowledge in such matters.

"William remembered everything the other children said to him, be they friends or enemies. He remembered things they were good at. He remembered birthdays and middle names and even the names of people they talked about. His mind was like a catalogue." George recovered his composure and told Bess that every single person in the village remembered Billy.

"Many of them I've now had long conversations with and they all say that he helped them!"

"Yes, I'm aware of the impact he's had. However, I'm intrigued to know what you have discovered."

"I will convey all my discoveries and before the piece appears in the newspaper, I will let you read it all."

"Thank you."

The two of them discussed the writing and drawings from the shed before going inside to look at the items still hanging on the walls. One of many that caught the attention of George was a piece called 'The Hand That Signed the Paper'. George recognised the title and, as the decorated piece was framed, he unhooked it and began to read the somewhat untidy writing.

"That's the only piece in here that is not original," said Bess.

"That's interesting," said George as he finished reading. "I know the piece, it's Dylan Thomas isn't it?"

"Yes. Now with the war it has even greater significance. William brought that with him when he arrived. It had already been framed. Now I can feel like I'm giving you something new. You see, William's father informed us about this poem in a letter when he began to understand the talents of his 8 year old son. They had listened to the Dylan Thomas broadcast and, that evening, William went upstairs and wrote out the four verses. It's not exactly the same, but it's close."

The third meeting happened a week later and George had been trying to gather information about school.

"Like I've said, I can only tell you how I see it. With some things, it is my interpretation and with others, it is facts."

Bess was trying hard to be as clear as possible with George and by this stage had introduced her opinions instead of simply relaying facts. Billy had a relationship with his teacher that was built only upon tolerance. Bess was the only one to be aware of the conversation between Billy and his teacher until today. Bess considered Billy to be a genius and was aware that this was not something that anyone would take seriously, coming from her. She told George that Billy spoilt any chance of full recognition for his abilities within the classroom with his honesty.

"The teacher had called William into his office to be reprimanded for writing poems in a mathematics lesson," Bess explained. "It would appear that he was most curious about the extra-curricular activity. He was very impressed and had asked which book it was from."

George was now anticipating every word of the explanation but reserved a little caution. Bess continued:

"The teacher, his name was Albert, asked William,
"Where did you learn these words?"
William was an overly-honest boy with little grasp of subtlety. He said "It's all my own work, I made it all up in the lesson." Albert was astonished."

George asked for a cup of tea in a forthright manner that Billy might have adopted. As Bess turned her chair and left the room to fulfil the request, George utilised the time he had gained for himself to think. George was desperate to see the poem but was realistic enough to know that it likely no longer existed in any physical form. He was also uneasy at the sudden amount of detail in the story despite Bess not being present at the meeting between child and headmaster.
As Bess walked in with the tea, George continued the conversation with a carefully prepared statement.

"You refer to the headmaster by his first name. You have clearly met him." George was fully aware that the use of a first name in this instance didn't represent a mere formal meeting. The break in proceedings had served George well. Bess gathered a few thoughts and became a little more open with the writer.

"I've met him several times," she said. "He called me to his office after the incident but he..." The pause was too much for George to follow his rule of silence in such circumstances.

"What!?" he said, knowing that there was so much more to the story.

"The last time I saw Albert was about five years ago, here." She said in a breath that was filled with a feeling of submission and relief. Bess went on:

"Albert discussed the meeting with Billy and was clearly angry and yet was also impressed with the poem. The problem arose when he'd asked Billy about a particular line." George asked if she remembered the line and was shocked but thrilled by the answer.

"Oh yes, I remember the whole poem," she said, "well not to the exact word, maybe. It went 'He lives in a room in the basement of his life' I think. Albert asked William if the poem was autobiographical and he told him 'Oh no Sir, it's not about me, it's about you'. I regret how that turned out for him. Not for Albert though, he retired a year later and moved to the village. He lived out his life serving the community. He died two years ago."

George was happy to have a minute or two and drink the tea. It resembled a minute's silence but he had no idea whether they were remembering the dead or not. Bess had taken a long time to open up and George wasn't about to push too hard.

Deciding not to pursue the story in the direction of Albert for now, George enquired about the poem and asked if Bess had it written down anywhere. Bess revealed an overdue smile filled with pride but also with relief and went into the extension. Returning with a framed drawing, she handed it to George who had the feeling of a historian discovering treasure. Below the drawing of the old school and gardens was the poem:

> *He lives in a room in the basement,*
> *Of a house that is his life.*
> *He was born but is yet to wake.*
> *And discover his brilliant mind.*
> *He waits for the drops of rain for the seeds.*
> *And not the start of his dreams.*
> *Of golden fields of brown dry wheat.*
> *Starved of light, the helpless seam,*

To sell their fields for golden beads.
Grand and fantastic in a Titanic way,
And will ask for rain but if there isn't any,
The plants will die, starved of opportunity.
The wheat that survives will sell itself.
And the weaker will not.
Birds that fly away.
Birds that have no flight.
And birds that lie dead, in the earth.
This eagle, crested and great.
Black wing-spanned, he could soar superbly.
But just marches by and sours unearthly.
Sets his standards with a cold, glass eye.

George was taking time with each line and was only half way through when Bess, for once, volunteered some important information, unprompted:

"He came to see me. Albert. A few weeks after, when the school was running only the one classroom in the basement. He asked about Billy with genuine concern".

George, now losing control of himself again, interrupted.

"Where was Billy!?"

"He was in the shed and when he saw the car, he walked off to the village, straight over the wall as he so often did. Albert spoke again about the poem and I could sense that he was trying hard to change. That's when he handed me the piece of paper and I saw the drawings with the poem."

Bess took a moment before adding:

"I told Albert that the garden of the school in the drawing was actually our garden. Albert knew of Billy's love of growing seeds but of course wouldn't have known that Billy had drawn his own garden beside the drawing of the school. The last time I saw him, he told me there was a typed version of the poem on his wall."

George was engrossed in the story to the point that his writing of notes had stopped. He was aware that Bess would provide no information when he first met her and it took a second meeting before anything was written down at all, but now George sensed that he could wait in the silence for Bess to reveal more.

"I think he came over to express his admiration for the poem and for William. In his office, when we first met, he asked if William had chickens! He also asked if we had a watering can for the garden. I think he was still hopeful that the poem was at least partly autobiographical. I told him that we had one but it had a leak. Well, I couldn't believe, when he walked out of the house and got a new watering can from his car!"

> *To skip or trip to the pond, tear-shaped and open for inspiration.*
> *Rain cries down onto the water and the winded, bloody leaves of autumn.*
> *The voice of God in its present time and virtue has fallen.*

On the occasion of George's final visit before publication of the article, he told Bess that he'd located Jack in a nearby town working as a carpenter. This had added to the story somewhat and George's notebook was a reflection of this but he still had some outstanding questions in his book. Bess said she was looking forward to the article and was happy to see it go ahead without her reading it first, but would love to read through the notes before George left. George agreed that this should happen.

"You know," said George in a rather rehearsed manner, "there are stories about what happened to William." Bess fully utilised her right to silence and speaking only when she had something to say. After all, it wasn't even a question.

"About the ice. He was last seen on the frozen water. Are you aware of those stories?" came the inevitable question.

"Of course I am. The water froze only one day that month, just at the edge," said Bess, with a hint of finality. However, after a long pause that George had learnt to ignore, she went on: "They say that John, from the village, saw him there. His work friend, Roger said he left him at work before making his way home. But they searched the water."

"Yes," said George, now believing that Bess was to reveal all she knew. "They didn't find anything. It was in the papers 3rd December 1945. Do you think he drowned there?" George knew this was the most important moment of the whole investigation.

"No!" said Bess, "No, I don't".

"Yet you never saw him again? He wouldn't just leave you, would he?"

"Let me see those notes," said Bess.

Bess read the notes.

Where is Jane? Nobody knows where she's gone! John, Robert, Mary? Not Mary.
Jack: "Billy is a legend! The bullies and the teachers merely helped to create it. Time and the sheer desperation of regret that we didn't appreciate him at the time make him a legend. He's gone and that's added to what he left behind." Heard they 'moved away'? When told his aunt is still there: looks amazed! He must have known?

Alfie (King's Arms): Listen to John! Others come over. It's all too much for some. Some say he's dead and some don't. Story about his day at school, punished for poems instead of verbs. 'I wish I'd gone over there.'

Was Margaret West the one who exposed Billy's visits to the village? Definitely his influence! Margaret has drawings of Billy's. Seem new! Has Wizard of Oz original press! 40 years old? Dog named Dorothy after the lead character.

'Oh the cows they happily lay
But to the milk house they go to 'prey'

But left, they would know the true way'

'People here assumed he was from the town, not from the countryside. The farmer gave him away and Bess had a visit from the vicar!'

'You can see into everyone's eyes. It's never dark. I'd prefer the old gas lights, you can turn up the light.' Billy's words saved by Florence. Brother-University.

Barbara: One day, that shed should be a museum. 'It' gets bigger every year.
Quotes in the post office.
In the library: framed on the wall, 'The Snow' by William Thomson! Name change?
'Friends will come and go
Like beautiful, early winter snow
I will help clear the way
Help to see and to grow
Until after I'm betrayed
Take my stories and conversations
Build your own and pass on your revelations'

A man was in the village asking where Billy was. He was a stranger and someone saw him talking to Billy after work. "The next day we heard about the ice. We never saw him again."

Bess stopped reading after the first page. She closed up the book and read no more.

"I spent five months believing that he was in the shed!" said Bess, both surprised and amused at her naivety but also struggling to take in the information that she had just read.

"I still don't know when he started going to the village, but it doesn't matter now."

So, I will go out onto life's thin ice, to create for you, a sacrifice

A copy of the newspaper arrived in the post. Bess read the article in the kitchen after noticing that it was part one of a series. With a range of expressions on her face, she read it right through. She read it through again and stopped regularly to think and to look out to the shed and garden. She was very happy with it and placed it carefully on her favourite book shelf. George had placed a note inside saying that he would visit again just to catch up on things. He also wrote a quotation from one of Billy's many poems: 'So I will go out onto life's thin ice. To create for you, a sacrifice.'

It was almost a month before George came back. He was looking content and relaxed. Bess had read the full series that he'd sent her and felt that he now truly understood the story of her beloved nephew. They talked about each other's lives for a while, now that George had the time for such conversation. George noticed some framed photographs that were not previously there. One was Billy with Dorothy and another was a very young girl. He admitted to discovering some new information but was in no mood to ask any more questions. George approached matters by informing Bess that he knew she was very wealthy and that her family of farmers had paid for her medical treatment as well as providing a good income. As Bess was no longer defensive with such developments, George went on to tell her that he knew her family had bought shares in a publishing business eight years ago. He had no idea what was to come from this confession.

"The article will now be made into a book," George informed Bess with a large amount of satisfaction and excitement. Bess appeared very happy with this news and chose the moment to open up.

"I expect a free signed copy to be sent to me, with the full author's name, Joseph George Brown. Or can I call you 'Joe'?" George took a moment to absorb the disclosure and then, assisted by the hint of a smile from Bess, he smiled contentedly.

"I did some investigating myself a while ago," clarified Bess.

"I knew him a little, all those years ago," said George. "Now I feel like I know him completely. I can't bring him back but I can bring back his story!" he said.

"Together, we could do both, maybe. I'm sure you'd get a lot more material. You set out to reveal all and you've revealed the roots of a very large tree." said Bess, pointing her stick at a bookshelf that appeared different from before.

"You have new books?" asked George.

"I just hid them away while you were here, that's all. No offence. Those 12 books, all different authors. Well, different names," said Bess, eager to explain something of their significance before George reached them.

"There are all kinds of things, from poetry and philosophy to children's stories." Two by two, George took the books from the shelf and began to absorb information from each one. He was engrossed for five minutes by one book, called 'The Very Well-Articulated Lorry' before lifting his eyes upwards and breathing deeply.

"Astonishing. Beautiful," he said.

"That one is a children's book. I wish it was a true story," said Bess. George opened another.

"I recognise this one, I've seen the cover in a store somewhere," he said.

"That one is based on a true story," carefully considering the extent of her disclosure. "It's about a young boy who uncovers a gangster plot after hearing a conversation in a graveyard." Bess enlightened George further about the content of the books while maintaining an increasingly thin veil over the authors.

"One of the authors is a brilliant poet, that's my favourite book of all the ones I ever read!" Feeling like he'd discovered some treasure, George was keen to read all the books but also to ensure many others do too.

"I'll be finding these when I get back to the city. I'll also be seeing the boss about them, if that's alright with you?" Bess had a look of warm and proud satisfaction, but also a degree of inevitability.

"Oh of course. I understand completely," she responded with a distinct whisper to indicate some desire for confidentiality.

"I will keep you informed throughout. I would of course, love to stay in touch anyway," said George.

Bess looked at the books with a smile.

"So would we!"

Blank page for comment / creation:

Blank page for comment / creation

The Author:

'These works were created between April 2020 and April 2025. The early works, such as 'The Penguins' were written during the early lockdown, solely for my own enjoyment of the creative process and I feel I have managed to maintain that approach through to the final piece, 'Ghost Writer'. The story, 'Seed Sower' spanned the period December 2020 to December 2024. This is an indication of the approach taken, whereby I have written only when I have felt inspiration and been able to produce my best work. The same principle has applied to my painting. Most of the artwork is in a cupboard, a few pieces are on the walls of relative's houses and five pieces are included in the book and on the cover.

The vast majority of the work has never been read by anyone at time of publication. I retired from teaching in October 2022 with the intention to publish the material I had at the time. However, it transpired that my priorities remained to continue with the creative process and this lasted for two and a half more years, leaving me with work scattered around the house on pieces of paper or in the notes in my 'phone or hidden in files on the laptop.

The book was a way to bring it together as well as to feel proud to hold it all in my hand as a final product. I like to think that, true to the Oscar Wilde definition of an artist, I have continued to create material, not to supply a demand, but solely for the creative process and personal enjoyment it generates.'

Printed in Great Britain
by Amazon